Essential Documents
for Saving Tax
2009/10

DOWNLOAD ZONE FOR BOOKS

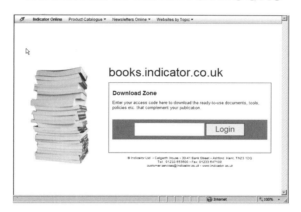

books.indicator.co.uk

Download Zone

Enter your access code here to download the ready-to-use documents, tools,
policies etc. that complement your publication.

Login

® Indicator Ltd · Calgarth House · 39-41 Bank Street · Ashford, Kent, TN23 1DQ
Tel. 01233 653500 · Fax. 01233 647100
customer.services@indicator.co.uk · www.indicator.co.uk

Go to
http://books.indicator.co.uk

and enter your access code
MGF438

for instant access to all the ready-to-use documents, tools, policies, etc.
that complement this publication.

Introduction

Tax is a difficult subject to deal with at the best of times. To make matters worse, the tendency to label everything "tax avoidance" means that it is now even more essential to have the correct paperwork in place to defend your position. The Taxman won't let you claim that a particular tax exemption applies or that your intentions were other than tax avoidance if you don't have the paperwork to prove it. Paperwork is essential in keeping the Taxman off your back. Should you find yourself on the end of a routine enquiry, it's a safe bet that the first thing he will want to see is your paperwork. And although the Taxman may start his initial enquiries into your current year returns, he can then go back over the last six years of returns and records. So getting the paperwork right now will stand you in good stead for the future.

For this reason, we decided to produce Essential Documents for Saving Tax. It includes over 100 letters, policies and checklists which cover all areas of taxation. It is divided into ten chapters which cover everything from company cars to VAT. Each chapter is accompanied by a useful commentary which describes how and when each document should be used. And with the complementary Download Zone website you can copy or adapt and print each one to suit your needs.

Ideally this book should become a useful companion and help you stay one step ahead of the Taxman. If you would like to see other documents added, please contact us and we will endeavour to include them in future editions.

Tony Court
Editor-in-Chief
August 2009

Table of contents

Chapter 1 - Profit extraction

Chapter 2 - Employee remuneration

Chapter 3 - Employee benefits and expenses

Chapter 4 - Company cars and vans

Chapter 5 - Status

Chapter 6 - VAT

Chapter 7 - Capital Gains Tax

Chapter 8 - Property investment

Chapter 9 - Inheritance Tax

Chapter 10 - Dealings with the Taxman

Chapter 1

Profit extraction

Distributable profits board minute

Once you've made a profit the challenge is getting it out of your company in the most tax efficient way. Paperwork to prove you had sufficient profits to pay a dividend is essential.

A LEGAL DIVIDEND

Company law says that once you've established the availability of distributable profits you can pay a dividend. These come in two types, interim and final. The directors have the power to pay an interim dividend if justified by profits. A final dividend must be proposed by the directors and approved by the shareholders. The Taxman can challenge payments described as dividends if they have not been declared and paid in accordance with company law. Indeed, if the directors allow a dividend to be paid when there are not enough retained profits it will be treated as illegal. To record the directors' proper consideration, use our **Distributable Profits Board Minute**.

DISTRIBUTABLE PROFITS BOARD MINUTE

There was then produced to the meeting [interim] accounts. The chairperson confirmed that the interim accounts had been prepared in accordance with the Company's normal accounting policies. The directors then considered the [interim] accounts and it was noted that the amount of profits available for distribution shown was £ . . . . . . *(insert figure)*.

The directors concluded that the [interim] accounts enabled them to make a reasonable judgement as to the amount of the distributable profits of the Company. It was noted that as the proposed dividend is to be paid immediately, the directors would not be required to undertake a further assessment of profitability except to the extent that were aware of any matters which might result in the Company making a loss. It was considered that there were no such matters.

The directors considered carefully the effect the dividend would have on the Company's ability to pay its debts as they fall due. To assist the directors there was produced to the meeting details of the Company's [cash flow] projections [and] [its current bank overdraft facilities]. It was noted that even after payment of the interim dividend, the Company would continue to have the resources to meet trading debts as they fell due.

Interim dividend board minute

A dividend is the most tax efficient way of getting money out of your company. However, you'll need a document to prove to the Taxman when the dividend was declared rather than let him choose a date that suits his tax take.

WHEN WAS IT TAKEN?

For a comprehensive board minute concerning all possible factors to be taken into account in proving that a payment to you was in fact an interim dividend see our **Interim Dividend Board Minute**.

The board minute details when the meeting took place and the total interim dividend proposed, with consideration for the distributable profits of the company and the effect the dividend would have on the company's ability to pay its debts as they fall due.

INTERIM DIVIDEND BOARD MINUTE

.... *(insert name of company)* Limited

Minutes of a meeting of the board of directors of .... *(insert name of company)* Limited held at .... *(insert venue)* on .... *(insert date)* at ..... *(insert time)*.

Present	Name	Position
Apologies for absence received from	**Name**	**Position**

1. Chairperson

.... *(insert name)* was appointed chairperson of the meeting.

2. Notice and quorum

The chairperson reported that due notice of the meeting had been given and that a quorum was present. Accordingly, the chairperson declared the meeting open.

3. Minutes of the meeting held on

The chairperson reported that the minutes of the board meeting held on ..... *(insert date)* were correct and that no other issues arose from those minutes.

4. Proposed interim dividend

4.1. The chairperson reported that [the meeting had been called because the Company had been requested by its shareholders to consider the payment of an interim dividend out of the profits available for distribution] [the business of the meeting was to consider, and if thought appropriate approve, the payment of an interim dividend to the shareholders of the company.]

4.2. It was noted that the Company's Articles of Association allowed the directors to pay interim dividends [only if it appeared to them that those dividends were justified by the profits of the Company available for distribution].

5. Proposed dividend

5.1. The chairperson then reported that the directors being asked to consider the proposal for the Company to pay an interim dividend for year of £.... *(insert figure)* per ordinary share at a total cost of £..... *(insert figure)*. If the directors resolved to pay the dividend it would be paid [immediately] to the member(s) whose names appeared on the Company's register of members at the time of the resolution.

5.2. There was then produced at the meeting a copy of the annual accounts for the Company for the period ended ..... *(insert date)* [which had been laid before the members in general meeting][had been sent to members][and contained an unqualified report from the Company's auditors].

5.3. The directors noted that the accounts showed profits available for distribution of £..... *(insert figure)*.

5.4. It was confirmed that [no dividends] [dividends in the sum of £ ..... *(insert figure)* had been paid since the balance sheet date of ..... *(insert date)*] [all the distributable profits shown in the Company's most recent annual accounts had been distributed to member(s)].

5.5. It was reported that the distributable profits of the Company as determined by the relevant items shown in the accounts [after taking into account distributions made since balance sheet date of..... *(insert date)* were such as would] [would not] justify the payment of an interim dividend of £ ..... *(insert figure)* proposed.

5.6. [There was then produced to the meeting [an individual profit and loss account and balance sheet showing profits, losses, assets and liabilities capital and reserves of the company as at ..... *(insert date)*] [interim accounts]. The [chairperson] [finance director] confirmed that the interim accounts had been prepared in accordance with the company's normal accounting policies [and the Company's auditors had confirmed that it was appropriate for the directors to rely on interim accounts].]

5.7. [The directors then considered the interim accounts and it was noted that the amount of profits available for distribution shown in the interim accounts was £........ *(insert figure)*. [It was explained this included ...... *(insert details of anything material, for example interim dividends from subsidiaries)*.]

5.8. Having discussed the interim accounts and asked any questions, the directors concluded that the interim accounts enabled them to make a reasonable judgement both as to the £..... *(insert figure)* of the distributable profits of the Company and as to the £..... *(insert figure)* of each item to which it was their duty to have regard in determining the profits available for distribution. It was noted that as the proposed dividend is to be paid immediately, the directors would not be required to undertake a further assessment of profitability except to the extent that they were aware of any matters which might result in the company making a loss. It was considered that there were no such matters.

5.9. The directors considered carefully the effect the dividend would have on the Company's ability to pay its debts as they fall due, having regard to the entirety the Company's business and the actual and contingent liabilities (future and present inherent in that business). [To assist the directors there was produced to the meeting details of the Company's [cash flow] projections [and] [its current bank overdraft facilities.] [It was noted that the [finance director] had confirmed that even after payment of the interim dividend, he was of the view that the Company would continue to have the resources to meet trading debts as they fell due.]

5.10. [To further assist the directors, the chairperson reported that . . . . . *(insert name of holding company)* had written to the Company giving confirmation to the effect that as long as the Company remained within the . . . . . *(insert name of holding company)* group of Companies . . . . . . *(insert name of holding company)* would use all reasonable endeavours to seek to ensure that the Company continued to be able to meet its foreseeable debts as they fall due; and if at any time the . . . . . *(insert name of holding company)* sold the Company to a third party it would not do so without endeavouring to obtain similar assurance from the third party concerning the Company's ability to meet foreseeable debts.]

6. Resolutions

After further discussion, it was resolved that;

6.1. The directors, having satisfied themselves that its payment would not affect the Company's ability to pay its foreseeable debts as they fell due, a dividend of £ . . . . *(insert figure)* . . . . . *(insert figure)* pence per ordinary share at a total cost of £ . . . . . *(insert figure)* dividend be paid [immediately] [on . . . . . *(insert date)*] to the member(s) of the Company whose name(s) appear on the register of members at the time of the resolution.

6.2. The payment of this dividend was to be satisfied using the available cash resources of the Company satisfied by drawing down on . . . . . . *(insert details of any loan facility with the bank)* [and/or left outstanding on intra group loan account].

6.3. [. . . . . *(insert directors' names)*]

[The company secretary] be and hereby authorised to take all the steps necessary to ensure payment of the dividend.

7. Close

There was no further business and the chairperson declared the meeting closed.

. . . . *(insert signature of Chairperson)*

Chairperson

. . . . *.(insert date)*

Dividend voucher

It's a good idea to issue dividend vouchers for any dividend payment from a company, regardless of its size. This is so that the shareholders can complete their tax returns accurately, thereby robbing the Taxman of a reason to open an enquiry into their return.

ISSUE A VOUCHER

To keep the Taxman at bay, it's a good idea to issue a **Dividend Voucher** after each dividend (interim or final). An alternative to this is to have it "approved" at the next meeting so that the company secretary will only have to issue one dividend voucher at the end of each tax year.

DIVIDEND VOUCHER

..............................(insert company name)

Directors: ....(insert name)

..............................(insert name)

..............................(insert name)

..............................(insert date)

..............................(insert shareholder's name)

..............................(insert shareholder's address)

....

Dear ....(insert shareholder's name)

Dividend for the period ending ....(insert your financial year-end)

I give below the details of the dividend payment made to you on ....(insert date).

Number of shares: ....(insert number of shares) ordinary shares of £ ....(insert nominal value) each.

Dividend rate: ....(insert percentage or pence per share)

Total dividend for the period ending: ....(insert date)

Total tax credit: £ ....(insert figure)

Note. Tax Credit is dividend paid x 10/90, e.g. on £900 the tax credit would be £100. You don't have to do anything with this other than record it on the voucher.

Remember to keep this voucher with your tax records. It supports the dividend entries you make on your self assessment tax return.

Yours sincerely

On behalf of ....(insert company name)

..............................(insert signature)

[Company secretary/director]

Dividend waiver

Broadly, a dividend waiver involves a shareholder waiving their entitlement to the dividend before the right to it has accrued. A dividend waiver can therefore be used as a way of reducing the income a higher rate tax-paying shareholder receives from the company. However, the timing of the document is crucial.

No DIVIDEND, THANK YOU

When a company pays a dividend, all the shareholders receive a cheque in proportion to their shareholding in the company. It's a case of all or nothing. Plus, under present rules, anyone liable to the higher rate of tax suffers an additional income tax on dividends. In other words, if you are already a higher rate taxpayer the problem with taking an extra dividend is that you pay tax on it. Yet fellow shareholders may have no tax to pay. This is where dividend waivers come in.

They can therefore be used as a method of reducing the income a shareholder receives from the company. You cannot waive the dividend after you obtain the right to receive it. Use our **Dividend Waiver** agreement to achieve this.

One possible use of a dividend waiver would be to divert income to one or more of the other shareholders. Make sure the dividend declared per share times the number of shares in issue does not exceed the amount of the company's distributable reserves.

DIVIDEND WAIVER

By this my deed dated . . . . *(insert date)*, I . . . . *(insert full name)* hereby irrevocably waive my entitlement to (the final/interim/any)* dividend arising on my entire holding of ordinary (or, if other, specify type) shares in . . . . *(insert company name)* from this day for EITHER:

(A) a period of maximum: 364 (three hundred and sixty four) days,

OR

(B) based on the accounts for the period ended . . . . . *(insert date)*

Signed . . . .

(Shareholder)

Full Name. . . . .

In the presence of:

Signature of witness. . . . .

Full Name. . . . .

Address . . . .

. . . .

Occupation . . . .

*   delete as necessary

the dividend(s) to be waived should be payable within 364 days of the date of deed. This option allows a more restricted waiver confined to only one dividend if required.

A deed should be prepared and reviewed by a solicitor.

Year-end bonus board minute

Bonuses for employees or directors declared after the year-end may only be accrued in the balance sheet if there was a "legal or constructive obligation at the balance sheet date" to make such payments. All other bonuses declared after the year-end cannot be included in the accounts until the following year.

BEFORE THE YEAR-END

It's common tax planning to prepare a draft set of accounts, work out the tax liability and then decide to vote a bonus to the directors (which must be paid within nine months of the year-end). This bonus is then included in the accounts to either clear an overdrawn director's loan account or reduce the company's Corporation Tax liability.

So you'll need to get an agreement in place before the year-end to pay bonuses after the year-end so they can still be provided for in the accounts. This condition can be easily satisfied by preparing a **Year-end Bonus Board Minute** before the company's year-end setting out the basis for determining it (e.g. x% of profits).

YEAR-END BONUS BOARD MINUTE

.... *(insert name of company)* Limited

Minutes of a meeting of the board of directors

Held at .... *(insert location)*

On .... *(insert date)* at .... *(insert time)*

Present	Name	Position

Apologies for absence received from	Name	Position

1. Chairperson

.... *(insert name)* was appointed chairperson of the meeting.

2. Notice and quorum

The chairperson reported that due notice of the meeting had been given and that a quorum was present. Accordingly, the chairperson declared the meeting open.

3. Minutes of the previous meeting

The chairperson reported that the minutes of the board meeting held on . . . . *(insert date)* were correct and that no other issues arose from those minutes.

4. Resolutions

It was resolved that:

4.1 The director(s) will receive a bonus based on the results of the Company at . . . . *(insert year-end date)*. The bonus will be calculated as . . . . *(insert details, e.g. as x% of profit)*.

4.2 The payment of this bonus will be made once the accounts have been finalised.

5. Close

There was no further business and the chairperson declared the meeting closed.

. . . . *(insert signature of Chairperson)*

Chairperson

. . . . *(insert date)*

Director's loan account record

When your company borrows from a bank it must pay interest on the money advanced. If you have a director's loan account with the company that's in credit, i.e. the company is holding money due to you, you are effectively lending money to it. Ask the company to pay you interest on the credit balance.

PAY THE INTEREST

If there is a **Director's Loan Account Record** with the company that is in credit, i.e. the company is holding money that is due to the director, interest can be paid on the outstanding balance. The company can pay a commercial rate of interest, which may be 5% or 6% above the bank base rate.

The interest can be paid by cheque or electronic transfer to your personal bank account or credited to your director's loan account, and on any other funds you have lent to it (thereby increasing the balance owed by the company to you). The payment can be made on a regular basis, either monthly and quarterly, or annually if you wish. However, as the company has to tell the Taxman how much interest it has paid to you each quarter, maybe it's convenient for it to pay interest due to you on the same basis.

DIRECTOR'S LOAN ACCOUNT RECORD

Company name: ....

Director's name: ....

Subject: *Record of transactions going through my director's loan account*

Date of transaction	Description of the transaction	Your initials	Amount In ("+") £0.00	Amount Out ("-") £0.00	Balance £0.00
X	Final dividend voted	X			
X	Interim dividend proposed	X			
X	Loan account interest due	X			
X	Rent due	X			

Interest payable on loan account minute

If you ask the company to pay you interest on the credit balance of your director's loan account, and any other funds you have with it, it's best to set out the terms and conditions of this arrangement by recognising it in the board minutes.

A COMMERCIAL RATE

It's best to set out the terms and conditions of this arrangement to prove that there is an obligation on the company to pay this interest by recognising it in the board minutes; use our **Interest Payable on Loan Account Minute** to do this. This allows the company to provide for the interest in its accounts and get a tax deduction for it, even if some of it's unpaid. The company should pay a commercial rate of interest for the money it has borrowed from you. This may be 5% or 6% over the bank base rate. However, if the company pays more than a commercial rate, the Taxman may view the excess as a payment of salary and require the company to deduct income tax and NI from it.

INTEREST PAYABLE ON LOAN ACCOUNT MINUTE

Board minute

The director(s) . . . . *(insert name(s))* has/have requested that the Company pay interest at a commercial rate of interest on his/their director's loan account when it is in credit. Having discussed the matter, the Board has resolved that the Company will pay interest on his/their loan account(s) at the rate of . . . . % *(insert figure)* above bank base rate per annum, to be credited to the loan account on the first day of each quarter based on the average balance outstanding in the previous quarter.

Annual certificate of interest

When you receive interest on your savings from a bank or building society it will issue an annual certificate of interest to help you put the correct entries on your tax return. If your company has paid you interest for lending it money, e.g. keeping a credit balance on your director's loan account, then why shouldn't it also issue you with an annual certificate?

HELP WITH TAX AFFAIRS

The interest can be paid or credited to the director's loan account on a regular basis to be drawn against later. Generally, the company has to deduct income tax at the rate of 20% from interest paid to the director. The company has to tell the Taxman how much interest it has paid each quarter (using a form CT61) and pay over any tax deducted. This form needs to be completed and submitted to the Taxman within 14 days of the quarters that end on March 31, June 30, September 30 and December 31. So quarterly is probably a convenient time to put the transaction through the company's books.

In order to help the director with their tax affairs at the end of the tax year the company issues an **Annual Certificate of Interest**.

ANNUAL CERTIFICATE OF INTEREST

.... *(insert company name)*

.... *(insert company address)*

....

....

.... *(insert name of director)*

.... *(insert address of director)*

....

....

....

.... *(insert date)*

Dear .... *(insert name of director)*

Interest Certificate for the period April 6 .... *(insert year)* **to April 5** .... *(insert year)*

Below is the interest you earned for the last tax year, which was paid to you or credited to your loan account.

Interest Before Tax   £ .... *(insert figure)*

(Gross Interest)

Tax Paid   £.............. *(insert figure)*

Interest After Tax   £.............. *(insert figure)*

(Net Interest)

Please note that any tax deducted was paid direct to the HMRC. The amount of interest actually paid to you or added to your account was the interest after tax.

Tax return. Remember to keep this certificate with your tax records. It supports interest entries you make on your self assessment tax return.

Yours sincerely

......................................*(insert signature)*

[Company secretary/director]

On behalf of ....*(insert company name)*

Licence agreement

If your company makes a payment to you in return for being allowed to use property you own, how can you make sure that the Taxman won't try to tax this as if it were an additional salary?

USE AN AGREEMENT

If you call the payment "rent" you can treat it as a separate source of income on your tax return and your company can claim a tax deduction for this expense. The property may be a commercial or domestic building, land, or even part of a building. On a smaller scale, even if your company uses the garage attached to your home, e.g. to store stock, you can let it out and receive rent in return. As long as the property is used by the company for its business, it can deduct the full cost of the rent paid from its profits.

You can charge the company as little rent as you wish for using your property. It does not have to be market value but it must not exceed it. The rent should normally be under a formal lease agreement between you and the company. This lease will stipulate how often rent should be paid, either monthly, quarterly or annually. If this is just an arrangement between a director and the company for using part of their home as an office then use our **Licence Agreement**.

LICENCE AGREEMENT

This agreement is made on . . . . *(insert date)* between

(1) . . . . *(insert company name)* (the "Company") and

(2) . . . . *(insert property owner's name)* (the "Property Owners")

(3) . . . .*(insert property owner's name)* (the "Property Owners")

It is agreed that

1. The Property Owners jointly own . . . . *(insert address of the property)* (the "Property").

2. The Property includes accommodation and contains furniture ("the Home Office") which is available for use by the Company and which it is envisaged shall be used by the Company from time to time.

3. It is agreed that in consideration for its use of the Home Office (between the hours of 9am and 5pm), the Company shall reimburse to the Property Owners such proportion of any expenses they incur in providing it as is fairly attributable to the use of the Home Office by the Company including (but without limitation) provision of broadband facilities, a proportion of mortgage interest, heating and lighting costs, maintenance and repair. The proportion is to be agreed between the parties from time to time having regard to the actual use made by the Company of the Home Office.

Signed on behalf of the Company . . . .

Name (in capitals). . . . .

Position . . . .

Signed by the Property Owners (1) . . . .

Signed by the Property Owners (2) . . . .

Date . . . .

Licence agreement (garage)

You might have already thought about charging your company for the use of your office at home. But what about situations where it is effectively using your garage as a storage facility? Can it get a tax deduction if it pays compensation for this convenience?

COMPANY STORAGE

If you have to use your own garage for company storage, can you claim rent in addition to that charged for using your home as an office? Yes. However, you will need to record any payment made to you by your company for use of your garage as such, both in your company's books (as an expense) and on your own tax return (as income). However, on your personal tax return you now get to claim for any additional costs of meeting your company's requirements for safeguarding those items (stock, records etc.) that are in your garage. Here's eight to get you started: **(1)** some products must not be exposed to high or low temperatures, so a proportion of household electricity costs to cover use of a heater (winter) or a fan (summer) in the garage should be claimed; **(2)** any storage boxes/cages; **(3)** additional insurance premiums; **(4)** security measures; **(5)** additional lighting; **(6)** weather proofing; **(7)** smoke alarm, fire extinguisher, sand bucket (particularly for chemical spills) etc.; and **(8)** the cost of a trolley to move products to and from the car/van - health and safety must be observed at all times.

Back this up with a **Licence Agreement (Garage)** between you and your company setting out the terms and conditions.

LICENCE AGREEMENT (GARAGE)

This agreement is made on . . . . *(insert date)* between

(1) . . . . *(insert company name)* (the "Company") and

(2) . . . . *(insert property owner's name)* (the "Property Owners")

(3) . . . . *(insert property owner's name)* (the "Property Owners")

It is agreed that

1. The Property Owners jointly own . . . . *(insert address of the property)* (the "Property").

2. The Property includes accommodation and contains an area ("the Garage Storage") which is available for use by the Company and which it is envisaged shall be used by the Company from time to time.

3. It is agreed that in consideration for its use of the Garage Storage, the Company shall pay the Property Owners rent. This rent is to take account of a proportion of the Property Owners' expenses incurred in providing it, as is fairly attributable to the use of the Garage Storage by the Company including (but not limited to) a proportion of mortgage interest, heating and lighting costs, maintenance and repair. The proportion is to be agreed between the parties from time to time having regard to the actual use made by the Company of the Garage Storage.

4. The Property Owners to take such steps as are necessary for the items stored not to be exposed to extremes of temperature whilst within the Garage Storage.

5. The Property Owners to put suitable security and fire prevention measures in place to reduce the risk of loss of items held in the Garage Storage.

6. The Property Owners to put such procedures in place that will allow the Garage Storage to comply with the Company's health and safety policy.

Signed on behalf of the Company . . . .

Name (in capitals) . . . .

Position . . . .

Signed by the Property Owners (1) . . . .

Signed by the Property Owners (2) . . . .

Date . . . .

Pro forma invoice

As an individual, you can sell an asset such as a building, a vehicle or other goods that you own to a business. When you sell it how can you prove to the Taxman that this was done under normal commercial terms, thereby preventing him from inserting his own (possibly) higher value for the deal?

MARKET VALUE

When you sell a capital asset to the company there is no NI to pay on any profit you make. The first £10,100 (2009/10 figure) of capital gains you make is also tax-free. Plus there's no tax to pay when you sell an asset that is exempt from Capital Gains Tax to the company, e.g. a car. When you sell a non-exempt asset you are taxed as if you sold it at market value, however much you actually receive for it. So it's important to obtain a market value for the item at the date of transfer.

To prove the sale details, raise a **Pro Forma Invoice** from you to the company, and have it entered in the company's books and records.

PRO FORMA INVOICE

INVOICE

. . . . *(insert your name)*

. . . . *(insert your address)*

. . . .

. . . .

. . . . *(insert telephone / fax number)*

. . . . *(insert e-mail address)*

. . . . *(insert date)*

. . . . *(insert name of company)*

. . . . *(insert address of company)*

Details	Amount (£)
Total due	

Spouse's job description

**A business can pay a salary to the spouse or other family member
of its owner if they work for it. Indeed, it's still possible to reduce the
owner's salary and pay a little more to the family member to reduce
the total amount of income tax and NI that the family as a whole pays.
But how much and how do you justify this amount to the Taxman if he
challenges it?**

PAY A SALARY

The wages paid to a spouse will be a valid tax deduction for the business if the Taxman is happy
that they are paid at a commercial rate for the work performed. First assess exactly what your
partner does for the business. Use our example of a **Spouse's Job Description** to help you record
their responsibilities. Next, calculate the average number of hours spent by your spouse per week
or month on business activities. This can be tricky, but even a rough diary note made at the time
is good evidence should the Taxman ever seek to challenge the amount paid. If your business is
run through a company you should check that the gross wage you expect to pay to your spouse/
partner is at least £5.73 per hour worked, which is the current National Minimum Wage (NMW).
(This will rise to £5.80 in October 2009.) Unincorporated businesses that pay family members who
live at home do not have to worry about the NMW. Remember, for the business to be guaranteed a
tax deduction, the wage must actually be paid rather than just made as an accounting adjustment
in the books.

SPOUSE'S JOB DESCRIPTION

1. Credit control clerk

Job title	Credit control clerk
Accountability	Accounts manager
Location	Main office (at your office address)
Brief description	To maintain and monitor 150 credit accounts
Duties and responsibilities	Cash allocation on computerised system Debt collection via telephone and standard letter Liaison with debt collection agency Some attendance at county courts Attendance of local credit meetings Maintaining credit limits Processing credit applications including credit checks Liaising with sales team
Hours of work	20 hours per week (flexible overtime may be required)
Rate of pay	£5.73 per hour (minimum)

2. PA role

Job title	Personal assistant (PA)
Accountability	Managing director (MD)
Location	Main office (at your office address)
Brief description	Work closely with the MD to provide day-to-day administrative support

Duties and responsibilities	Screening telephone calls, enquiries and requests and handling them if they do not think it necessary to pass on to their manger
	Organising the MD's diary
	Making appointments
	Dealing with incoming e-mail, faxes and post
	Taking dictation
	Writing letters and reports
	Carrying out background research into subjects the manager is dealing with, and presenting findings in an easily digestible form
	Standing in for the MD in their absence
	Organising meetings
	Liaising with clients, suppliers and other staff
	Making decisions and delegating work to others when the manager is unavailable
	Devising and maintaining office systems to deal efficiently with paper flow, and the organisation and storage of paperwork, documents and computer-based information
	Taking responsibility for recruiting and training junior staff and delegating work to them
	Arranging travel and accommodation
	Travelling with the MD from time to time, to take notes at meetings, take dictation and provide general assistance in presentations
Hours of work	20 hours per week (flexible overtime may be required)
Rate of pay	£5.73 per hour (minimum)

Director's loan account write-off letter

The classic solution to clear any director's overdrawn loan account is to pay the money back to the company, or more usually, to take extra remuneration from the company in the form of dividends or bonuses. However, it could instead write the loan off, if it gets the paperwork right.

CLEAR THE ACCOUNT

You don't have to actually pay a dividend to clear a loan account because s.421 of the **Taxes Act 1988** says that if a loan of this type is discharged or written off by the company, then it is treated in the same way as if it were a dividend (a deemed dividend) paid to that individual. Using s.421 the other shareholdings are irrelevant; what matters is the amount being written off. The director's deemed dividend would need to be included on their personal tax return and the company has to write to its Corporation Tax office about what has been done. You can use our **Director's Loan Account Write-off Letter** to do this.

DIRECTOR'S LOAN ACCOUNT
WRITE-OFF LETTER

. . . . *(insert date)*

HMRC

. . . . *(insert company's tax office)*

Dear Sirs

. . . . *(insert company name) (insert tax reference)*

During the above financial year, the company discharged loans on behalf of . . . . *(insert number of directors)* of its directors under s.421 **Income and Corporation Taxes Act 1988** as follows:

. . . . *(insert name of director)*   NI number: £ . . . . *(insert amount)*

. . . . *(insert name of director)*   NI number: £ . . . . *(insert amount)*

   £ . . . . *(insert amount)*

We would refer you to paragraph 6663 of the HMRC Company Taxation Manual and confirm the amounts are to be treated as net distributions under Schedule F. The gross amounts will be included in the directors' individual self assessment returns as dividends for . . . . *(insert year)*.

Yours faithfully

. . . . *(insert signature)*

. . . . *(insert company name)*

Director's loan agreement

A director/shareholder does not normally have to sign a loan agreement when they borrow money from their company. However, if they are not the only shareholder, company law states that they should get written permission from the other shareholders before they borrow the money. An agreement setting out the key terms will help you with any queries from the Taxman.

A DEEMED DIVIDEND

A director's loan account can be written off by the company, and treated in the same way as if it were a dividend (a deemed dividend) paid to that individual. The director's deemed dividend would need to be included on their personal tax return and the company has to write to its Corporation Tax office about what has been done. However, it's best to formalise the loan in advance by getting a **Director's Loan Agreement** drawn up and a company minute authorising the write off. This helps if there are any queries raised by the Taxman in the future.

DIRECTOR'S LOAN AGREEMENT

THIS AGREEMENT is made on . . . . *(insert date)*

BETWEEN

(1) . . . .*(insert name of company)*
of . . . . *(insert address of company)* ("the Lender"); and

(2) . . . .*(insert name of director)*
of . . . .*(insert address of director)* (the "Borrower").

The Lender has been requested to make a loan to the Borrower which the Lender has agreed to do upon the terms and conditions which follow.

1. Amount of loan

The Lender will lend to the Borrower and the Borrower will borrow from the Lender the outstanding balance on the Borrower's loan account with the Lender ("the Loan") on the terms which follow.

2. Interest

The Borrower shall pay to the Lender interest on the Loan at the rate of [NIL%] [. . . . . *(insert figure)*] per annum quarterly on the last day of each of the months of [March, June, September and December] [January, April, July and October] [February, May, August and November] in each year. The first such payment to be made on whichever of the interest payment dates first occurs after the advance of the Loan and to be in respect of the period from and including the date of such advance until the next interest payment date.

3. Repayment

Unless otherwise agreed, the Borrower may only repay the Loan by a single payment on . . . . . *(insert date)*.

4. Compulsory repayment subject to demand

The Lender may, by notice in writing to the Borrower, demand the immediate payment of all moneys due or incurred by the Borrower to the Lender together with all interest and any other sums forthwith (or otherwise as the Lender may require) at any time if the Borrower does not pay on the due date any money which may have become due hereunder or under any document supplemental hereto.

5. Compulsory repayment without demand

All moneys and obligations due or incurred by the Borrower to the Lender shall become immediately due and payable on the happening of any of the following events:

(a) the death or bankruptcy of the Borrower;

(b) if a petition is presented for an administration order to be made in relation to the Borrower pursuant to the **Insolvency Act 1986**;

(c) if any secured creditor or encumbrancer takes possession or a receiver (which expression shall include an administrative receiver as defined by the Insolvency Act 1986) is appointed of all or any part of the property and assets of the Borrower.

6. Interpretation

Covenants, warranties and undertakings given by an individual shall be binding on his personal representatives and executors.

7. Governing law

The Law of England shall apply to this Loan and the parties submit to the jurisdiction of the English courts.

EXECUTED as a deed on the day and year first above written.

EXECUTED as a DEED by   )

[The Lender]   )

in the presence of   )

Signature of witness . . . .

Name of witness . . . .

Address . . . .

Occupation . . . .

EXECUTED as a DEED by   )

[The Borrower]   )

in the presence of   )

Signature of witness . . . .

Name of witness . . . .

Address . . . .

Occupation . . . .

Benefit-in-kind paperwork

You can get your company to pay for certain personal expenses and get a tax deduction for it if you include it as part of your negotiated remuneration package. What paperwork do you need on file to support this?

PART OF YOUR PAY PACKAGE

If your company pays, say, for a room in your house to be decorated, what documentation do you need to make sure it gets a tax deduction for this as a legitimate part of your remuneration package? Firstly, you'll need to get formal **Benefit-in-kind Paperwork** drawn up which demonstrates to the Taxman that the benefit was agreed by the company as a way of rewarding you for your services to the company. There is no need for any special wording, just a statement of the facts as a record for future reference. Secondly, because this is a variation of your remuneration package, you will need to incorporate it into your contract of employment by way of an addendum to the main contract. Thirdly, getting the provider of the service to invoice the company will make it absolutely clear that the liability for payment belongs with the company and not you. And fourthly although there are no special disclosure requirements, if you include the charge for the service to remuneration costs, it reinforces your position that it's part of your pay package.

BENEFIT-IN-KIND PAPERWORK

1. **The board minute.** Remember that any expense charged in the Company's accounts has to meet the "wholly and exclusively" test for the purpose of the trade. Getting a formal board minute drawn up demonstrates to the Taxman that the benefit was agreed on by the Company as a way of rewarding you for your services. There is no need for any special wording, just a statement of the facts as a record for future reference.

   Example:

   "Meeting of the Board of Directors of XYZ Limited on . . . . . . (insert date and time) at . . . . (insert location).

   It was resolved that the Company approve the payment of Mr X's . . . . (insert details) as part of his remuneration package.

   This award has been made in recognition of his continuing contribution to the success of the company.

   Signed . . . . (insert name) company secretary"

2. **Your contract of employment.** Because this is a variation to your remuneration package you will need to incorporate it into your contract of employment by way of an addendum.

   Example:

   "As of . . . . (insert date) the Company will contract and pay for . . . . (insert details) subject to the availability of funds. This benefit-in-kind is to be treated as part of your remuneration package with the Company."

Chapter 2

Employee remuneration

Salary sacrifice letter

If you currently pay all of your employees' salaries as cash, then real savings can be made if they sacrifice part of it for a non-taxable benefit such as pension contributions, childcare vouchers or even additional holiday.

BENEFIT-IN-KIND

Remuneration can take the form of cash, which will always be fully taxable if it is for duties performed in the past, present or future, or as a benefit-in-kind, which may or may not be taxable. The ideal situation is to provide a benefit that is tax deductible for the employer, and generates neither an income tax charge for the employee nor an NI charge for either of you. It is essential that you get your employees to sign a **Salary Sacrifice Letter** before the reduced salary is due to take effect, otherwise the Taxman will insist that they are taxed on the benefit as if it were pay.

SALARY SACRIFICE LETTER

. . . . *(insert name)*

. . . . *(insert address)*

Date . . . . *(insert date)*

Dear . . . . *(insert name)*

Consent in Relation to Deductions from Salary

Please note that with effect from . . . . *(insert date)* your basic salary will be reduced by . . . . . . *(insert amount)* from . . . . . . *(insert amount)* to . . . . . . *(insert amount)*. The sum of . . . . . . *(insert amount)* is to be:

[paid into the Company's pension scheme for your benefit upon retirement*]

[paid as childcare vouchers*]

[paid as . . . . . *(insert details of benefit)*]

[In addition, you have elected to take . . . . . . *(insert amount)* additional holidays and, therefore, your basic salary will be reduced by a further . . . . *(insert amount)* (i.e.1/260th of gross salary per additional holiday day taken) to . . . . . . *(insert amount)*.]

Your notional salary (which will form the basis of any future salary reviews) will be your gross salary at your last salary review.

These new agreed terms represent a permanent variation to your contract of employment. The Staff Handbook sets out the rules for the scheme and you must read it carefully before signing the attached copy of this letter and returning it to . . . . *(insert name)* to signify your agreement to the changes and deductions detailed above.

Yours sincerely

_____

I have read the scheme rules as set out in the Staff Handbook and agree to the changes and deductions outlined above and acknowledge that these new agreed terms represent a permanent variation to my contract of employment.

* delete as appropriate

. . . . *(insert signature)*

. . . . *(insert date)*

Salary sacrifice policy

If you want to implement a salary sacrifice scheme in your company, make sure you insert the relevant policy in your staff handbook. Your policy will need specific details regarding extra holiday or pension provision.

SCHEME PARTICULARS

Including a **Salary Sacrifice Policy** in your staff handbook is important both to convey the details of the scheme and to point out any drawbacks. For example, a sacrifice requires a permanent alteration to the employment contract and could have an effect on borrowing capacity for mortgages and credit cards as well as possibly interfering with benefits and work-related payments such as Statutory Maternity, Adoption, Paternity or Sick Pay.

SALARY SACRIFICE POLICY

The Company offers a salary sacrifice scheme, whereby it can [pay your pension contribution directly into your pension scheme] and/or [you can "buy" additional holiday*] and/or [provide you with childcare vouchers*] in exchange for a salary sacrifice. This saves both the Company and you from paying NI contributions (and in some instances, tax) upon the salary that you sacrifice.

Details are as follows: . . . . *(insert salary sacrifice policy - holidays and/or pensions and/or other details).*

Scheme rules

Each participant in the scheme will be notified of a notional salary that will form the basis of any future salary reviews.

The Company reserves the right to withdraw the salary sacrifice scheme at the end of the Company's financial year which runs from . . . . . . *(insert start date)* to . . . . . . *(insert end date).*

Gross salaries will be adjusted from the date of joining the salary sacrifice scheme onwards.

A sacrifice must not cause the rate of pay to be less than the prevailing minimum wage figure.

Drawbacks of salary sacrifice

As the sacrifice is a permanent alteration to the contract of employment, you will not have the right to revert to the original (higher) salary level; otherwise the sacrifice will not be valid in the eyes of the HMRC and if they deem the sacrifice to be ineffective for any reason, then the contribution will be treated as a benefit-in-kind and could therefore increase tax and NI liabilities rather than reducing them.

However, in exceptional circumstances, if you are forced to revert to the original (higher) salary level, this can only be done via a mutually agreed variance of your contract in writing and cannot be subsequently rescinded. Such action may affect the taxation consequences of the original salary sacrifice as explained above. Applications must be made in writing to . . . . *(insert name).*

It must be remembered that, as the name of the salary sacrifice scheme suggests, salary must be genuinely sacrificed, therefore any other benefits or transactions which are based on salary or the amount of NI contributions made will be affected. For example:

Any borrowing levels, such as mortgage, credit card limits, personal loans etc., which are set in conjunction with the salary level, will be affected by the sacrifice.

Contribution-based state benefits such as Incapacity Benefit, Job Seekers' Allowance and State Pension will be affected by any salary sacrifice, as will earnings related benefits such as Maternity Allowance and, where the revised salary falls between the Lower Earnings Limit (LEL) and the Upper Earnings Limited (UEL), the State Second Pension.

Work related payments such as Statutory Maternity, Adoption, Paternity or Sick Pay will also be adversely affected by a sacrifice. If the sacrifice reduces the salary to less than the LEL then entitlement to Basic State Pension would be affected.

Working Tax Credit and Child Tax Credit could also be affected by any sacrifice.

delete as appropriate

Sample childcare voucher

You can sacrifice part of your salary for childcare vouchers to save on tax and NI. For a fee, you can use a childcare voucher company to administer the scheme for you, but there's nothing to stop you printing your own vouchers and issuing them to employees.

TAX-FREE VOUCHERS

The first £55 per week of childcare vouchers that you give to an employee is both tax and NI-free. By offering employees the opportunity to take a pay cut in exchange for childcare vouchers, you will save the 12.8% employers' NI and the employee will save both tax and NI. Use our **Sample Childcare Voucher** as a template for your own vouchers. The employee can use the vouchers to pay for approved childcare, e.g. a registered childminder. They give the voucher to the approved child carer who then sends it back to you for the company to settle.

Note. The £55 limit is per parent not per child so if both parents work in the same company, they can receive up to £110 a week tax-free (via separate vouchers).

SAMPLE CHILDCARE VOUCHER

Front of voucher:

Childcare Voucher	Childcare Voucher	
		Valid only in the UK
(Insert employee's name)	Value:	**£(insert amount)**
(Insert employee's number)	**(insert employee's name)**	
(Insert employer's contact address)	Valid until:	**(insert date)** *(valid for 12 months)*
	(insert your company name and address)	_____ Childcarer's signature
Value: **£(insert amount)**		Childcarer's name *(please print)*
	_____ Employee's signature	_____ Childcarer's registration number
Voucher No:	Voucher No:	

Reverse of voucher:

Conditions of Acceptance

Voucher validity:

1. Valid until the last day of the month printed on the front of this voucher
2. This voucher may only be used by a legally entitled person/childcare

For further information contact the customer services organisation department on

(insert telephone number)

Notice to childcare provider:

The employee must sign the front of the voucher and the childcare provider must counter sign the voucher before it will be paid.

Completed forms should be returned to

(insert your company name and address).

In the UK this voucher remains the property of *(insert your company name)* and is not transferable *(insert company address)*

Issued by:

Address:

Childcare voucher policy

Where childcare is provided by way of voucher, the first £55 per week is tax-free if certain conditions are met. Whether you administer a voucher scheme yourself or engage an external voucher provider, what evidence do you need in place to demonstrate that your scheme meets the requirements?

AN APPROVED SCHEME

To meet the Taxman's conditions for tax-free childcare, you will need evidence that the scheme is offered to all employees, so include a **Childcare Voucher Policy** in your staff handbook.

Our policy sets out two major conditions of the scheme. Firstly, that the child must be the employee's child or stepchild and is living with them with parental responsibility for that child. Secondly, that the voucher must be used to pay for qualifying childcare by a registered childcare provider. Be aware that certain exclusions exist to prevent particular types of care from qualifying. Relief will be denied if the care is provided: **(1)** by the employer's partner; or **(2)** by a relative of the child, wholly or mainly in the child's home. A relative is a parent, grandparent, aunt, uncle, brother or sister *"whether by blood, half blood or civil partnership"*.

CHILDCARE VOUCHER POLICY

The Company operates a childcare voucher scheme which is open to all employees. The scheme is implemented as a salary sacrifice arrangement where you exchange part of your salary for childcare vouchers.

The first £55 per tax week of the voucher's face value will be given to you tax and NI-free as long as the following conditions are met:

Condition A:

- the child must be your actual child or stepchild and be maintained (wholly or partly) at your expense or

- the child must be living with you and you have parental responsibility for the child.

Condition B:

Childcare vouchers can only be used to pay for any form of qualifying childcare. Qualifying childcare includes:

- registered childminders, nurseries and play schemes

- school or council-run out of hours clubs

- extended school scheme run by school governing bodies

- childcare schemes run by approved providers

- childcare given in the child's home by an appropriate registered agency worker

- approved foster carers (but not for their own foster children).

Childcare provided by a relative of the child wholly or mainly in the child's home does not qualify even where the childminder is registered.

Procedure

You will provide details of your childcare provider to the Company including their registration or approval number together with the date the relevant registration expires.

You must notify the Company of any changes in registration or approval status of your child's carer or changes in childcare arrangements.

The Company will provide you with a childcare voucher. You will then give this voucher to your qualifying childcare provider. The childcare provider will then sign the voucher and send it to the Company for reimbursement. There is no cost to the childcare provider in receiving payment through childcare vouchers.

Register of child carers

The Taxman imposes quite an onerous record-keeping burden on employers when it comes to childcare. In particular, for the £55 per week relief to apply the care must be "qualifying childcare", defined as registered or approved care. How should you go about checking this and recording the results?

STRINGENT RECORD KEEPING

The HMRC Employer Helpbook E18 - "How to help your employees with childcare" indicates that you will need to keep the following:

(1) A copy of your scheme rules that includes a requirement for employees to notify you of any change in circumstances in relation to the child or childcare.

(2) A record of the childcare provider's name and registration or approval number.

(3) A note of when the childcare provider's approval is going to expire.

According to guidance in E18, the following websites can provide information on whether a particular carer is registered or approved: in England, http://www.ofsted.gov.uk or alternatively http://www.dcsf.gov.uk/everychildmatters; in Scotland http://www.childcarelink.gov.uk; in Northern Ireland, local health and Social Services Trusts http://www.dhsspsni.gov.uk; and in Wales http://www.wales.gov.uk.

To comply with the age restriction requirements (a person is considered a child until the Saturday after September 1 following their 15th birthday), you also need to keep a record of the date of birth of an employee's youngest child.

Use our **Register of Child Carers** to keep detailed records of all the carers involved with your childcare voucher scheme.

REGISTER OF CHILD CARERS

Employee name	NI number	Date of birth of youngest child	Name of childcare provider	Address 1	Address 2	Address 3	Postcode	Telephone number	Registration number	Date of expiry of registration

Personal appreciation gift letter

There are a few circumstances in which an employee can receive tax-free cash from an employer. But a gift made "on personal grounds" or as a "mark of appreciation" might be one of them. How do you go about proving this to the Taxman's satisfaction?

A PERSONAL GIFT

Where cash paid to an employee is a genuine gift in recognition of some personal quality, and is in no sense a reward for performing duties past, present or future, then it can be paid tax-free. The Taxman's instructions suggest that to escape liability, possible reasons for the gift might be: "on personal grounds, e.g. a wedding present, or as a mark of personal esteem or appreciation". Always keep a copy of the covering letter with any such payment to provide evidence, if required, to the Taxman. Our **Personal Appreciation Gift Letter** will serve this purpose.

PERSONAL APPRECIATION GIFT LETTER

. . . . *(insert date)*

Dear . . . . *(insert employee name)*

We would like to make a cash gift to you of . . . . *(insert amount)*. This gift is in recognition of . . . . *(insert reasons for payment)* and is not in any way related to your employment duties. In accordance with the **Income Tax (Earnings and Pensions) Act 2003**, it is treated as a tax-free honoraria payment. If you need to complete a tax return, this payment should be entered under "any other income" but in the additional information box, you should refer to it as a "tax-exempt honoraria payment".

Yours sincerely

. . . . *(insert signature)*

Staff suggestion scheme rules

You might want to reward your employees for certain ideas that contribute to the success of your business. Previously by concession, this is now a statutory exemption. However, there are conditions you'll have to meet.

FINANCIALLY BENEFICIAL

A little-known way of giving employees tax and NI-free cash is through a staff suggestion scheme. The scheme needs to be formally set up, but that doesn't take much doing. You tell the staff that they will receive a small payment in return for ideas that may help the business. A really good idea that is taken up by the company will get a larger reward. Write down the amounts you plan to pay, and how you would like the ideas to be put forward. Pin these **Staff Suggestion Scheme Rules** to the office notice board so everyone can see them, and you are all set to start the suggestion scheme. You can pay up to £25 for any suggestion but if it is implemented and likely to financially benefit the company, you can pay out the lower of £5,000 and 50% of the expected financial benefit in the first year (or 10% of the expected financial benefit over five years).

STAFF SUGGESTION SCHEME RULES

1. The scheme is open to all employees on equal terms.

2. An award may be made, at the discretion of the board of directors (or by a committee appointed by the board), for a suggestion which is outside the scope of the employee's normal duties. In this regard, the test is whether or not the employee, taking account of his experience, could have been expected to put forward such a suggestion as part of his normal duties.

3. An encouragement award may be made in respect of a suggestion which, although it will not be implemented, has some intrinsic merit and/or reflects meritorious effort on the part of the employee in making the suggestion. The amount of such an award will not exceed £25.

4. Alternatively, an implementation award may be made directly to the employee(s) concerned, following a decision to implement the suggestion. The amount of any such award will be based on the degree of improvement in efficiency and/or effectiveness likely to be achieved, measured by reference to:

   - the prospective financial benefits and the period over which they are expected to accrue, and

   - the importance of the subject matter having regard to the nature of the Company's business

   and will not exceed:

   - 50% of the expected net financial benefit during the first year of implementation, or

   - 10% of the expected net financial benefit over a period of up to five years

whichever is greater.

5. Where a suggestion is put forward by more than one employee, any implementation award arising from it will be divided between them on a reasonable basis.

6. The scheme does not apply to any sums paid to an employee in respect of the exploitation or disposal of rights in an invention devised by them (such as patent rights, know-how, etc.)

7. The company does not guarantee to any employee that an award will be tax-free. However, any encouragement award under this scheme is likely to be non-taxable, as is the first £5,000 of any implementation award (divided as necessary between two or more employees where 5. above applies).

8. The decision of the board on the amount of any award, and on the terms of the scheme generally, shall be final.

Suggestion scheme ideas log

In certain circumstances tax rules permit employers to reward staff tax-free for ideas. But the Taxman will want to see some evidence of the benefit the business has derived from this payment. Is there a simple way of doing this?

Log the ideas

The really clever bit of a staff suggestion scheme is that even if you get snowed under with suggestions, you get to pick the ideas to be used or rewarded so you decide who gets the money. The Taxman, however, will want to know all about the tax-free amounts you are giving to your staff, so you need to estimate and record the cost savings or extra sales revenue for any suggestion that you use. Use the **Suggestion Scheme Ideas Log** for this.

SUGGESTION SCHEME IDEAS LOG

Employee name	NI number	Suggestion	Implemented (Y/N)	Estimated financial benefit to company	Amount paid* £

* The maximum you can pay for suggestions that are not implemented is £25. The maximum you can pay for implemented suggestions is the lower of £5,000 and 50% of the expected financial benefit in the first year (or 10% of the expected financial benefit over five years).

Golden hello payment letter

An inducement payment will sometimes be made to a new employee. Such a payment will normally be taxable. Exceptionally, it may be tax-free if you can demonstrate that the payment is not by reason of the employment. How can you establish this?

LUMP SUM PAYMENT

A "golden hello" is a popular term for a lump sum payment received on the taking up of employment. Normally, tax is due on these payments as if they were salary. However, if the payment is an inducement rather than a reward for future services, then it should be tax-free if it satisfies the following conditions:

- it must be clear from the facts that the payment is an inducement and not a reward for future services

- the payment must not be returnable if the person does not take up the employment

- from case law, it is more likely that the payment will be accepted as tax-free if the prospective employee has previously been self-employed and is giving up some right or asset to take up the employment.

Make sure the payment is accompanied by the **Golden Hello Payment Letter** which indicates that the payment is an inducement.

GOLDEN HELLO PAYMENT LETTER

. . . . *(insert prospective employee's name and address)*

. . . .

. . . .

. . . .

. . . . *(insert date)*

Dear . . . . *(insert name)*

Please find enclosed a payment of . . . . . . *(enter amount)* as compensation for giving up
. . . . *(enter details of right or asset given up)* and joining our company.
This is a one-off non-returnable payment and in no way represents reward for future
services. No tax has been deducted from this inducement payment as it falls outside the
provisions of s.225 **Income Tax Earnings and Pensions Act 2003**.

Yours sincerely

. . . . *(insert signature)*

Enc

Payment in lieu of notice clause

You might decide that an individual should not work out their notice period and that they should be paid for this period instead. You need to take account of the legal more than the tax issues when drafting documentation for dealing with a termination payment. So where should you start?

To use a **PILON** clause?

In the absence of an express **Pay in Lieu of Notice** (PILON) **Clause**, pay in lieu of notice will be regarded as a payment of compensation in connection with termination of employment, i.e. damages for breach of contract. With a PILON clause, pay in lieu of notice is regarded as wages payable under the contract of employment. So, why does it matter what it's classed as? Firstly, with a PILON clause, you can limit the amount payable, as our pay in lieu of notice clause does, to basic salary only. Where you have to pay damages for breach of contract, the damages must put the employee in the position they would have been had the contract been properly performed. This means you will have to compensate the employee for the loss of any benefits-in-kind during what would have been the notice period. Secondly, since without a PILON clause you are technically committing a breach of contract if you pay in lieu, there is a high risk that an employment tribunal will hold that you cannot then enforce the other provisions of the contract. If the contract contained restrictive covenants, this could cause you a major headache if you can't rely on them. Thirdly, the employee could try and bring a claim for wrongful dismissal against you if you have paid in lieu with no PILON clause, although if you have adequately compensated them for their loss, their claim may have little substance. And finally, the clause does not say you have to pay in lieu of notice - it only says that you may do so, so the choice is yours. You can still require the employee to work out their notice period even with a PILON clause.

PAYMENT IN LIEU OF NOTICE CLAUSE

The Company reserves the right to make a payment in lieu of notice for all or any part of your notice period on the termination of your employment. This provision, which is at the Company's discretion, applies whether notice to terminate the contract has been given by you or the Company. Any such payment will consist solely of salary and shall be subject to such deductions of income tax and NI as the Company is required or authorised to make.

Compromise agreement

If you breach the contract of employment to ensure that a payment in lieu of notice payment is tax-free, then it is a good idea to use a compromise agreement to prevent any claims against you.

NEGOTIATED TERMINATIONS

Sometimes, it will become necessary to dismiss an employee in circumstances where you want to prevent them from issuing employment tribunal or other court proceedings against you in relation to infringement of their statutory (or contractual) employment rights. This may happen in relation to senior employees when you do not propose to go through formal dismissal procedures because you want them out as soon as possible. In such circumstances, you should hold a "without prejudice" meeting to discuss the termination package in return for their signing a **Compromise Agreement**. This is essentially a formal, legally binding agreement made between an employer and employee (or ex-employee) in which the employee agrees not to pursue particular claims they believe they have in relation to their employment or its termination, in return for a financial settlement from the employer.

COMPROMISE AGREEMENT

THIS AGREEMENT is made on . . . . *(insert date)*

AND IS MADE BETWEEN:

. . . . Limited *(insert name of Company)* whose registered office is at . . . . *(insert registered office details)* ("the Company"); and

. . . . *(insert name of employee)* of . . . . *(insert address of employee)* ("the Employee")

RECITALS:

1. The Employee has been employed by the Company under the terms of a contract of employment dated . . . . *(insert date).*

2. This Agreement satisfies the conditions regulating compromise agreements under:
   - Section 203 of the Employment Rights Act 1996
   - Section 72 of the Race Relations Act 1976
   - Section 77 of the Sex Discrimination Act 1975
   - Schedule 3A to the Disability Discrimination Act 1995
   - Schedule 4 to the Employment Equality (Religion or Belief) Regulations 2003
   - Schedule 4 to the Employment Equality (Sexual Orientation) Regulations 2003
   - Schedule 5 to the Employment Equality (Age) Regulations 2006
   - Regulation 9 of the Part-Time Workers (Prevention of Less Favourable Treatment Regulations 2000
   - Regulation 8 of the Fixed-Term Employees (Prevention of Less Favourable Treatment Regulations 2002
   - Regulation 35 of the Working Time Regulations 1998
   - Section 49 of the National Minimum Wage Act 1998
   - Section 288 of the Trade Union and Labour Relations (Consolidation) Act 1992.

3. The Employee has received independent legal advice from a solicitor, ... *(insert name of solicitor)* of . . . . *(insert firm name)* of . . . . *(insert firm address),* as to the terms and effect of this Agreement and, in particular, its effect upon their ability to pursue their rights in an employment tribunal. By signing this Agreement, ... *(insert firm name)* warrants that the solicitor who provided the advice holds a current practising certificate and that the firm currently maintains the level of indemnity cover required of it by the Law Society covering the

risk of a claim by the Employee in respect of any loss arising in consequence of the advice they have received.

THE COMPANY AND THE EMPLOYEE AGREE AS FOLLOWS:

1. The employment of the Employee by the Company (will terminate/terminated) on .... *(insert date)* ("the Termination Date").

2. This Agreement is in full and final settlement of all employment related claims that the Employee has and/or may have against the Company whether or not they are or could be in the contemplation of the parties at the time of signing this Agreement.

3. The Employee has notified the Company that they consider they are in a position to make a complaint of .... *(insert details of employee's complaint, for example unfair dismissal, sex discrimination, race discrimination, etc. and refer to any correspondence in which the employee has notified the Company of their complaint).*

4. Neither the Employee nor the Company shall directly or indirectly make or otherwise communicate any disparaging or derogatory statements about the other, either verbally, in writing or otherwise, which might reasonably be considered to insult, damage or impugn their reputation.

5. The Company shall:

    5.1. Pay the Employee their salary up to and including the Termination Date and pay in lieu of any accrued but unused annual leave entitlement. These sums will be subject to normal statutory income tax and national insurance deductions.

    5.2. Without admission of any liability as claimed or otherwise, pay to the Employee by way of compensation for termination of employment the sum of £ .... *(insert amount)* within 14 days of the signing of this Agreement ("the Payment"). Of this sum, £ .... *(insert amount)* will be paid free of income tax and national insurance deductions pursuant to section 401 of the Income Tax (Earnings and Pensions) Act 2003 and the balance of £ ...... *(insert amount)* will be paid after the deduction of income tax and national insurance.

    5.3. Pay the Employee a sum in respect of .... *(insert number)* (weeks/months) pay in lieu of (contractual/statutory minimum) notice within 14 days of the signing of this Agreement ("the Pay in Lieu"). This sum will be (subject to normal statutory income tax and national insurance deductions/paid free of income tax and national insurance deductions as it does not represent contractual remuneration).*

    5.4. Pay the Employee a statutory redundancy payment of £ .... *(insert amount)*, paid free of income tax and national insurance deductions, within 14 days of the signing of this Agreement.*

5.5. Provide the Employee with a P45 within 14 days of the signing of this Agreement.

5.6. Continue, up to and including . . . . . . *(insert date)*, to provide the Employee with the benefits of (*life assurance, private medical insurance and pension scheme contributions) on the same terms as those benefits were provided to the Employee as at the Termination Date.*

5.7. Permit the Employee to retain their company car until . . . . *(insert date)* on the same terms and conditions as they enjoyed the use of that car during their employment but on the understanding that no mileage incurred by the Employee will constitute travel between their home and the Company's premises nor will it constitute business travel.*

5.8. Provide the Employee with a reference in the attached terms should the same be requested by any potential employer of the Employee.*

5.9. Contribute to the Employee's legal costs in seeking advice as to the terms and effects of this Agreement up to a maximum of £ . . . . *(insert amount)* plus VAT on receipt of an appropriate invoice in the Employee's name and marked payable by the Company and which refers to the advice.*

*(*Delete as appropriate.)*

6. The Employee shall:

6.1. Not divulge to any third party at any time any trade secrets or other confidential information belonging to the Company or any of its associated companies and not use such secrets or information for their own benefit or that of any third party.

6.2. Return to the Company all documents, computer hardware and software, keys, cards and any other property which belongs to the Company or relates in any way to the business of the Company or any associated company which are in their possession or under their control.

6.3. Refrain from disclosing the contents of the terms of this Agreement other than to their spouse, partner, lawyer or accountant except as may be ordered by any court, government agency or as required by law.

6.4. Accept full responsibility for the payment of any income tax and national insurance deductions not already made by the Company and indemnify and keep indemnified the Company against all and any liabilities to income tax or national insurance deductions which the Company may incur in respect of or by reason of the Payment or the Pay in Lieu and, within seven days of being informed by the Company of the amount of any such tax assessment, pay to the Company an equivalent amount.

6.5. Confirm that they have not at the date of this Agreement accepted, either verbally or in writing, an offer of employment or entered into a contract for services or a consultancy agreement with any person, firm or company.

6.6. Confirm that they have not knowingly committed any breach of duty to the Company, or any breach of the terms of their contract of employment.

6.7. Resign from their directorship (and as Company Secretary) with the Company with effect from the Termination Date, execute a letter of resignation in such form as the Company shall require and execute any further documents as may be necessary to give full effect to the resignation, including completing any formalities necessary to secure the amendment of records at Companies House.

6.8. Forthwith withdraw their employment tribunal claim number . . . . *(insert number)*.

6.9. Accept the payments and actions of the Company set out above in full and final settlement of all or any claims arising out of their contract of employment or its termination which they may have against the Company or any associated company or any of its or their officers or employees, whether such claims are known or unknown to the Employee and whether or not they are or could be in the Employee's contemplation at the time of signing this Agreement, and whether such claims are contractual, statutory or otherwise, including, but not limited to, claims for:

6.9.1. Damages for breach of contract (whether brought before any employment tribunal or otherwise) in respect of any salary, holiday pay, notice pay, bonus or commission due.*

6.9.2. Unauthorised deduction from wages under the Employment Rights Act 1996.*

6.9.3. Holiday pay under the Working Time Regulations 1998.*

6.9.4. Unfair dismissal, including constructive dismissal.*

6.9.5. Damages arising out of the Company's failure to deal with the Employee's grievance in accordance with the ACAS Code of Practice on Disciplinary and Grievance Procedures or the Company's grievance procedure.*

6.9.6. Damages arising out of the Company's failure to deal with disciplinary action against and/or dismissal of the Employee in accordance with the ACAS Code of Practice on Disciplinary and Grievance Procedures or the Company's disciplinary procedure.*

6.9.7. Detriment relating to the making of a protected disclosure under the Public Interest Disclosure Act 1998.*

6.9.8. Contractual or statutory redundancy pay.*

6.9.9. Discrimination by reason of sex, sexual orientation, race, religion or belief, age, disability or trade union membership or activity.*

6.9.10. Victimisation or harassment in connection with sex, sexual orientation, race, religion or belief, age, disability or trade union membership or activity.*

6.9.11. Equal pay.*

6.9.12. Less favourable treatment on account of being a part-time worker.*

6.9.13. Less favourable treatment on account of being a fixed-term employee.*

6.9.14. Any claim arising out of the transfer of an undertaking under the Transfer of Undertakings (Protection of Employment) Regulations 2006.*

6.9.15. . . . . *(insert details of any other claims raised by the Employee).*

(*Delete as appropriate.)

6.10. Accept that if their rights under any of the provisions referred to above have not been validly and lawfully excluded by the provisions of this Agreement and if they should purport to exercise such rights (or any of them) and if an employment tribunal or other court should find that any compensation is payable to the Employee by the Company as a consequence, the monies paid to the Employee under this Agreement shall be deducted (so far as may be requisite) from any award of compensation in diminution or extinction thereof.

SIGNED:

. . . .

Director

For and on behalf of the Company

SIGNED:

. . . . *(insert name of employee)*

SIGNED:

. . . . *(insert name of solicitor)*

For and on behalf of . . . . *(insert name of firm)*

Indemnity clause

Despite everything you've done, the Taxman might decide that your payment to the now ex-employee is not tax-free after all. If you are forced to pay the PAYE bill how can you reserve the right to recover this from the employee?

COVER YOURSELF

If you compensate an employee on termination of their contract, you should ask them to sign a Compromise Agreement. Within this agreement you should include an **Indemnity Clause**. This will typically provide that, although the payment is believed to be tax-exempt, if you are required to make payment of tax and NI to the Taxman in respect of the payment, then you can recover the money so paid from the employee.

INDEMNITY CLAUSE

The employee shall accept full liability for the payment of any income tax or NI deductions not already made by the Company and indemnify and keep indemnified the Company against all and any liabilities to tax or NI deductions which the Company may incur in respect of or by reason of the Payment.

Termination payment letter

You need to take account of both the legal and tax issues when drafting documentation for dealing with a termination payment. But if you don't have any employment issues with the departing employee it's arguable that the payment can be made tax-free (subject to the £30,000 tax-free limit). How can you improve your chances of the Taxman agreeing with you?

THE TAX-FREE LETTER

The major downside to having a **Pay in Lieu of Notice** (PILON) **Clause**, is that the payment is then taxable as it's a payment of wages made under the contract of employment. Without a PILON clause, it's arguable that the payment is tax-free (subject to the £30,000 tax-free limit) as compensation for loss of employment. If you don't have any employment issues with the departing employee you should enclose a **Termination Payment Letter** with the payment to the employee. This should explain that you have not made a payment in lieu of notice but have breached the employee's contract. It is therefore seen as damages for the breach. Further evidence that a termination payment is tax-free.

TERMINATION PAYMENT LETTER

. . . . *(insert name)*

. . . . *(insert address)*

Date . . . .   *(insert date)*

Dear . . . .   *(insert name of employee)*

WITHOUT PREJUDICE

In accordance with the compromise agreement dated . . . . . *(insert date)*, we enclose a cheque in the sum of . . . . *(insert amount)*. This ex gratia payment solely relates to compensation for termination of your employment and was not provided for in your employment contract. Of this sum, £. . . . . . *(insert amount up to £30,000)* has been made without deduction of income tax or NI. [The balance of £ . . . . . . *(insert amount over £30,000, if applicable)* has been paid with income tax and NI deducted as follows:

Gross payment	£.	*(insert amount)*
Income tax	£.	*(insert amount)*
NI	£.	*(insert amount)*
Payment enclosed	£.	*(insert amount)*]

Yours sincerely

. . . . *(insert signature and name of author)*

Enc

Termination payment minutes

You can use company law formalities to support your case that a termination payment is not ordinary earnings and hence not taxable (up to a £30,000 limit). What's involved?

Ex gratia minutes

If possible, agreement to make a termination payment, and its approval by the board using **Termination Payment Minutes**, should be made after employment ceases. Where this is not practicable, any reference in any minute or document should be as brief as possible and refer to the payment only as being "ex gratia". Don't refer to it as "consideration for past services" as this will almost certainly make it taxable.

TERMINATION PAYMENT MINUTES

. . . . *(insert company name)* LIMITED

MINUTES OF A DIRECTORS' MEETING

HELD ON . . . . *(insert date)*

IT WAS RESOLVED that following the termination of . . . . 's *(insert employee's name)* employment with the Company, a payment of £ . . . . . . *(insert amount)* should be made to them as compensation for breach of contract.

. . . . *(insert signature)*

Chairperson

Quality standard checklist

At the end of each tax year, you are required to complete the annual return Form P35 and submit it to the Taxman by no later than May 19. There are penalties if this form is rejected. How can you minimise the chances of this happening?

THE TAXMAN'S STANDARD

The Taxman issues a series of checks, which he calls the Quality Standard, which the P35 together with the corresponding P14, must satisfy before being accepted. If your return doesn't meet the Quality Standard, then it could be rejected, leading to a fine of up to £3,000. One of the new requirements is that you can no longer use temporary NI numbers on P14s. Use the **Quality Standard Checklist** to help ensure that your year-end returns comply with the Taxman's standard.

QUALITY STANDARD CHECKLIST

This checklist can be used whether you file online or submit paper returns.

1. If you are using payroll software, check with your software supplier that it meets the Taxman's Quality Standard.

2. Check that no temporary (usually starting with TN or 00) NI numbers are being used.

3. Where the NI number is not known, the field should be left blank and the employee's date of birth and gender entered.

4. Where both the employee's NI number and date of birth are unknown, enter 01.01.1901 in the date of birth field.

5. The employee's gender must be entered if they pay reduced rate NI or received SMP.

6. Entering the employee's private address is optional.

7. On P14s for employees earning less than the Lower Earnings Limit (£110 per week for 2010), "X" must be used as the NI category letter.

8. If the employee's NI category is F, G, H, K, S or V, then make sure a scheme contracted-out number (SCON) is included in the correct format, e.g. S 12345678A.

9. Check that the PAYE total on the P35 agrees with the individual P14s.

10. Check that the NI total on the P35 agrees with the individual P14s.

11. Do not include Class 1A contributions on the P35 end of year return. These must be reported separately on a P11D(b).

12. For all employees that are members of contracted-out pension schemes (i.e. NI category letters D, E, F, G, H, K, L, N, O, S or V) make sure the appropriate employers' contracted-out number (ECON) has been entered.

PAYE audit checklist

The Taxman has recently changed his approach to what he calls compliance visits. If he sends you a letter telling you he wants to carry out such an inspection, what's the best way to handle the visiting inspector?

PREPARE FOR A VISIT

The Taxman has a legal right to inspect your payroll records to confirm that you are paying the correct amount of tax and NI. He sees these visits as a chance to make some easy money. Most PAYE inspections result in some mistakes being found and the Taxman will usually calculate the "lost" tax and NI over a period of six years plus the current year. This period may even be extended if he suspects that tax has been withheld on purpose. He may also seek penalties, although these will normally depend on the size of the error and how much the employer co-operates. Use the **PAYE Audit Checklist** to help prepare for an impending visit.

PAYE AUDIT CHECKLIST

Before the visit

Contact the Taxman to arrange a specific time for the visit (if you can't make the dates he's suggested, offer an alternative within one month of the original).

Check that the following records are complete:

- PAYE
- hours worked, such as clock cards or timesheets
- cash book
- petty cash.

Print off hard copies of your payroll records, e.g. the P11s (you don't want the Taxman to have access to your computer files).

Review a sample of the records yourself. If you find any problem areas, seek advice from your accountant.

Arrange for a separate office to be available so that your visitors' movements are controlled.

Send a memo to all staff saying that the Revenue auditors are only doing their job and they are not trying to catch them out. Remember to leave a copy of this in the visitors' room.

During the visit

Collect all the records requested and place them in the visitors' room.

Ask to see the Taxman's official ID card on arrival and make a note of his name.

Give him your extension number so that all his queries and requests come straight to you.

Make sure your diary is clear for the day so that you can be available as and when required.

If photocopies are requested, get your own staff to do it. Get them to keep a record of what he's taken.

Disclose voluntarily, at an early stage, any known irregularities to demonstrate a willingness to co-operate.

Don't give an off-the-cuff answer if you're not sure of your facts. Don't speculate - if you don't know, say so.

Make notes during the visit of any answers given by you or your staff to ensure later correspondence can be checked against the facts stated during the visit.

Don't sign any statements during the visit - take time to check them thoroughly and have them vetted by an advisor, adding in anything necessary to clarify confusing points.

Chapter 3

Employee benefits and expenses

Expenses claim form

**You have an obligation to provide certain information regarding
benefits and expenses to the Taxman and to your employees.
However, it's not always enough to just collect the information - you
also need documentation to support the benefit or expense.
A good place to start is an expenses claim form.**

THE NEED TO KEEP RECORDS

At the end of each tax year, you need to prepare P11D forms for all directors plus employees earning more than £8,500 a year. Collecting and analysing the information for these forms can be an onerous task, and the cost of getting it wrong is potentially very high penalties.

Each employee who claims business expenses over the year should keep all their receipts which match the figures entered on the **Expenses Claim Form**. The procedures for submitting and authorising expense claims should be well documented and communicated to employees.

DISPENSATIONS

Analysing a year's worth of your employees' expense claim forms is a very time-consuming, but necessary, task in order to accurately complete the P11Ds (unless you have a dispensation in place). To apply for a dispensation, you need to complete the Taxman's form P11DX which can be downloaded at http://www.hmrc.gov.uk/forms/p11dx.pdf Once you've sent off the initial application, the Taxman will usually ask for a copy of your claim form.

EXPENSES CLAIM FORM

Date: . . . .

Employee's name: . . . .

Department: . . . .

Note: All claims must be supported by a VAT receipt/invoice

Date	Description	Total £	VAT £	Mileage £ (complete separate claim form)	Other travel £	Meals £	Accommodation £	Entertaining £	Other £

Total:

Signed by: . . . .

Authorised by: . . . .

Expenses policy

In order to a get a reporting dispensation from the Taxman, your procedures for the submission and authorisation of expense claims needs to be well documented and communicated to employees.

Evidence of a legitimate claim

In addition to the claim form, the Taxman will also ask for a copy of your **Expenses Policy**. He will grant a dispensation if he's happy that no tax will be payable by the employees on the expenses or benefits provided. He wants to know that you have a good system in place to ensure that only business expenses are being reimbursed before agreeing to a dispensation. Therefore, our policy covers all the rules and requirements for legitimate claims, such as prior authorisation and provision of VAT receipts. He will also want to see that the expense claims are always authorised by someone other than the claimant.

EXPENSES POLICY

It is the Company's policy to reimburse employees for all necessary travel, accommodation and other expenses, including the entertainment of clients, incurred while engaged on authorised Company business.

The Company will set levels of expenditure that are deemed appropriate and which may only be varied at the discretion of the Company.

The level of reimbursement allowed will be sufficient to provide a standard and quality which will adequately meet the needs of employees from the viewpoint of both comfort and acceptability for the effective conduct of Company business.

1. The rate of reimbursement is set at levels contained in the attached schedule and may only be varied at the discretion of . . . . *(insert name)*.

2. All expenditure must be authorised by . . . . . . *(insert name)* before it is incurred, to ensure that it is both necessarily incurred and reasonable.

3. Employees are required to provide VAT receipts covering all expenditure and without these, reimbursement will not be made.

4. Employees are required to apply for reimbursement by way of a written claim to . . . . *(insert name)* on a weekly/monthly* basis.

5. [Advances for anticipated expenditure may be applied for in the same way and must be accounted for properly.] *

    [Authorised employees who are required to entertain clients regularly on behalf of the Company or otherwise to incur expenses on the Company's behalf will be afforded the facilities for such expenditure, in the form of a credit card. Expenditure will remain subject to the specified Company limits and credit/charge card bills must be supported by receipts.] *

6. The expenses procedure will be monitored by . . . . . . *(insert name)*. Any abuse by employees will result in disciplinary action and, depending on the circumstances, is likely to be treated as gross misconduct resulting in summary dismissal (e.g. where an employee has intentionally sought to defraud the Company).

* delete as appropriate

Travel expenses policy

To a get a reporting dispensation for specific expenses (e.g. travel expenses) from the Taxman you'll need company polices which you can prove have been effectively communicated to your employees.

BUSINESS TRAVEL

Including a **Travel Expenses Policy** in your staff handbook will provide evidence to the Taxman that you only reimburse qualifying travel expenses. This will make him more likely to grant a dispensation for these expenses, reducing the amount of work you need to do at the year-end.

Our policy makes reference to home-to-office travel, which should not be included in business travel claims plus the type of transport which should be used on business trips. It specifies that the use of public transport as opposed to taxis should be used wherever possible. (Own car use is covered in a separate policy.)

TRAVEL EXPENSES POLICY

Business journeys

You can claim the full cost of any travel expenses incurred while you are on Company business.

Home-to-office travel

You are responsible for the cost of travel between your home and normal place of work. Costs relating to such journeys should not be included in claims for business travel expenses. When a business journey starts or ends at home, the amount claimed should be arrived at by deducting the normal mileage travelled to and/or from home and the office.

Travel by taxi

Use of public transport (bus, tube or train etc.) is encouraged and should be used wherever possible, for business purposes. However, it is recognised that the use of a taxi may, in the following circumstances, be the most effective mode of transport:

- where equipment or heavy baggage is being carried
- when no public transport is available, especially when travelling early in the morning or late at night
- when the claimant is pregnant or has a temporary or permanent disability
- where personal or financial security is an issue
- when it is important to save time
- when in an unfamiliar area and uncertain about public transport.

You should obtain an official receipt from the taxi driver to substantiate your subsequent travel expense claim, and you must state clearly on the expense form the reason for use of a taxi.

Travel by train

You are encouraged to take advantage of special deals where possible, and will be expected to travel in standard class. Expense forms must have attached to them as supporting documentation either the actual train tickets or a receipt from the train company. If a receipt is required, this should be requested at the time of ticket purchase as they are not usually given automatically.

Travel using own car

See separate policy.

Using your own car on company
business policy

If employees use their own vehicles for business journeys, you should have a company policy which spells out the situation regarding insurance, parking and mileage rates at which you will reimburse them.

TAX-FREE MILEAGE

Include the **Using Your Own Car on Company Business Policy** if employees use their own vehicles for business journeys. You will need to make it clear that it's the employee's responsibility to ensure they have adequate insurance in place and that the company will not be liable for any parking fines issued. Provided the reimbursement made to them is not more than the Taxman approved tax-free mileage rates, no benefit-in-kind will need to be reported on the P11D and it does not need to be included in a dispensation. However, the Taxman will expect you to keep a record of the amounts paid and the business journeys they are for.

USING YOUR OWN CAR ON COMPANY BUSINESS POLICY

Insurance

As the driver is personally liable for any incident, you should ensure that your own private motor vehicle policy is comprehensive and permits the use of your own vehicle for the purposes of business use. The cost of acquiring this is reflected in the mileage rate.

Mileage rates

The Company will reimburse you for business mileage at the following rates:

First 10,000 miles in a tax year - 40p per mile

Over 10,000 miles - 25p per mile

Mileage claims should be made at the end of each month by completing the mileage record form and expenses claim form.

Parking fines

Parking fines and other penalties will not be refunded by the company.

Mileage record

Any reimbursement for a journey that is ordinary commuting or non-business travel should have had tax and NI deducted, hence the Taxman's interest. If he starts asking questions about the accuracy of your business mileage, is there an easy way to satisfy his curiosity?

BUSINESS MILEAGE

If you can, provide a detailed mileage log of all business journeys. If you can't don't worry, because in practice, it's possible to get the Taxman to accept, albeit reluctantly, a sample log for a defined period, or indirect records, e.g. a diary showing the date and destination of journeys, from which mileage can be worked out.

Warning. He has been known to use web-based route finder services to check distances used in expense claims. So if you're not sure of the mileage, use one yourself.

Diaries/notebooks. You might have the mileage records in a diary or a notebook. It's best to transfer this to a mileage log showing the date of the mileage and the purpose of the trip - just in case there's anything else in the notebook that you wouldn't want the Taxman to see.

Generally. As the tax-free rates change depending on the number of miles completed in a tax year, you also need to have procedures in place to keep track of the number of miles claimed by each employee. One way of doing this is by getting employees to fill out a monthly **Mileage Record** in addition to their expenses claim form.

Name: ....

Month/year: ....

MILEAGE RECORD

Date	To	From	Reason	Miles	Claim
Business mileage brought forward for tax year to date				3,620	
1.1.09	Whichever town	Business base/shop/office	See X Client	10	£4.00
3.1.09	Whichever town	Business base/shop/office	Deliver X	15	£6.00
5.1.09	Whichever town	Business base/shop/office	See potential new client X	12	£4.80
6.1.09	Whichever town	Business base/shop/office	Networking breakfast/ lunch/ evening do	13	£5.20
6.1.09	Whichever town	Business base/shop/office	Visit suppliers	16	£6.40
8.1.09	Whichever town	Business base/shop/office	Visit accountant to discuss general business	18	£7.20
12.1.09	Whichever town	Business base/shop/office	Post office to post/stamps/stationery	3	£1.20
12.1.09	Whichever town	Business base/shop/office	Shops to buy X business items	5	£2.00
14.1.09	Whichever town	Business base/shop/office	Training update courses	95	£38.00
Total amount claimed					£74.80
Business mileage carried forward for tax year to date				3,807	

Notes

1. *Use the business mileage b/fwd where you make monthly claims to ensure you do not exceed 10,000 miles per annum limit.*
2. *Where business mileage is less than 10,000 miles per annum, the claim is up to 40p per mile.*
3. *Where business mileage exceeds 10,000 miles per annum, the claim is 25p per mile.*
4. *The reasons given above are just examples. You should record all travel that is undertaken for business purposes giving as much detail as possible to support your claim.*

Scale rate clearance letter

There's still a need for cash even in today's world of debit cards, company credit cards etc. If you want your company to pay you a regular cash allowance to cover your "expenses", how can you avoid paying tax on it?

ROUND SUM ALLOWANCE

Approach the Taxman for a dispensation to pay a "modest" round sum allowance to employees/directors in order meet non-receipted business expenditure. These amounts can then be paid tax-free.

SEND A LETTER

It's not uncommon for directors or employees to have a round sum allowance to cover such things as accommodation and subsistence. The allowance will be taxed as income, but a tax deduction may be claimed in respect of any part of the allowance which can be shown to have been spent on business purposes. It is very important to have a record-keeping system which enables such claims to be substantiated. To reduce the administration burden, get the Taxman's agreement in advance that these round-sum payments (scale rates) will be fully covered by business expenses by sending a **Scale Rate Clearance Letter**. He should agree as long as he is satisfied that the calculation of your scale rate is based on genuine expenses incurred in the past and there is no profit element in it for the employee. You will need evidence that supports the scale rate that you want to use. Average figures based on the last twelve months would be ideal, but even an average of the last three months (a weighting in favour of current prices) demonstrates that you haven't just plucked a figure out of the air. Don't send this with your initial letter though; keep it back until needed.

SCALE RATE CLEARANCE LETTER

HMRC

. . . . *(insert address)*

. . . .

. . . .

. . . .

. . . . *(insert date)*

Dear Sirs

. . . . ***(insert employer's PAYE reference)***

We intend to start making the following round sum payments to employees with regard to travelling and subsistence expenses:

Accommodation:

London	Per night, exclusive of meals	£75
	Per night, inclusive of meals	£96
Elsewhere	Per night, exclusive of meals	£60
	Per night, inclusive of meals	£85

Meals (when staying away overnight):

	Breakfast	£6
	Midday meal	£7
	Evening meal	£15

We do not consider that there is any profit element in the above rates. The rates are based on an accurate survey of the costs actually concerned and are reasonable in relation to the employment involved.

Under company policy, the employee will still need to fill out an expenses claim form before a payment is made.

We should be grateful if you would confirm that we can make these round sum payments without the need for them to be taxed under PAYE.

Yours faithfully

. . . . *(insert signature)*

Incidental overnight expenses policy

If an employee has to stay away overnight on business, there are some tax-free expense payments you can make. To achieve this you'll need to have a company policy in place to avoid an employee claming for the wrong amounts, which is what a visiting Taxman would come looking for.

EXPENSE PAYMENTS

If an employee has to stay away overnight on business, then you can pay them up to £5 per night in the UK (£10 per night overseas) tax-free, in respect of their miscellaneous personal expenses such as telephone calls home or newspapers. If you want to do this, you need to have procedures in place to make sure you don't accidentally reimburse the expenses twice - first as part of the hotel bill and second via the employee's separate expense claim. This can be achieved by following the **Incidental Overnight Expenses Policy**.

INCIDENTAL OVERNIGHT EXPENSES POLICY

Personal incidental expenses, for example, personal telephone calls, newspapers, laundry, etc., incurred whilst staying away overnight on Company business, must be excluded from the accommodation costs. They should be identified separately on the invoice by the hotel, or if this is not possible, highlighted by the claimant and excluded on the expenses claim. The Company will not reimburse invoices that do not show any personal expense items separately. The employee will be responsible for these costs.

The maximum amount that can be claimed per night on personal incidental expenses is equivalent to the HMRC's tax-free limits which are currently:

Staying away in the United Kingdom	£5.00 (inclusive of VAT)
Staying away overseas	£10.00 (inclusive of VAT)

The employee must reimburse the Company for any amounts in excess of these tax-free limits by July 6, following the tax year in which the overpayment occurred.

Overpayment of expenses policy

Annual reporting by employers of benefits-in-kind to the Taxman (on P11Ds) also doubles up as a requirement to report expenses payments to employees. The trap is that these are taxable unless the employee can claim a deduction for them. So accidental reimbursement of non-business expenses comes with a tax bill. How can you avoid this?

CLAIM THE EXPENSES BACK

Have a clear **Overpayment of Expenses Policy** so that you are entitled to claim any overpayment of expenses back from the employee before the next P11D is prepared.

These overpayments can be taken straight from the employee's salary. With round sum allowances, keep a record of who has them and how much they are for, what they are meant to cover and why they haven't been put through the payroll.

OVERPAYMENT OF EXPENSES POLICY

The Company reserves the right to make deductions from salary where there has been, for whatever reason, an overpayment of expenses. Overpayments will be recovered in accordance with the principles outlined below which apply to all staff employed by the Company.

Principles

1. Overpayments remain Company money at all times. They never form part of employees' salary or remuneration packages.

2. Overpayments will be recoverable direct from the employee's salary or wage.

3. It is the employee's duty to notify the Company if they believe an overpayment has been made.

4. Where the Company discovers an overpayment, the employee will be notified in writing, giving precise details of the overpayment.

5. Where an employee is leaving the Company, the overpayment must be repaid in full upon termination of employment. In these circumstances, the sum will be deducted from final pay due at termination, without prior agreement.

6. Where an overpayment is discovered following issue of final pay, the Company reserves the right to pursue recovery of any outstanding amounts through the courts.

PAYE settlement agreement letter

The point of a PAYE settlement agreement with the Taxman is that you (the employer) formally agree to meet the tax liability in respect of certain employee benefits/expenses that the Taxman has spotted. When would you actually need such an agreement?

TO MAINTAIN GOODWILL

Where you make a minor or irregular gift to an employee that gives rise to a tax or NI liability, you can use a PAYE Settlement Agreement (PSA) to pay any liability on behalf of the employee. The use of a PSA involves grossing up the payment for tax and NI so the value received by the employee represents the net value after deductions. This does make giving a free gift more expensive, but it will help to maintain staff goodwill - a gift isn't always so welcome if it comes with a large tax bill. The Taxman doesn't provide a standard application form, so to set up a PSA you need to write to your local inspector using the **PAYE Settlement Agreement Letter**, describing which gifts you want to include. If the item is subject to tax or NI at the time of making the gift, the agreement must be in place before the payment is made. In other cases, they can be agreed after the event. The tax due must be paid by October 19 following the year to which the PSA relates. A PSA has to be renewed on an annual basis but this is usually a formality.

PAYE SETTLEMENT AGREEMENT LETTER

HMRC

. . . .*(insert address)*

. . . .

. . . .

. . . .

. . . .*(insert date)*

Your ref *(insert your employer's PAYE tax reference)*

Dear Sirs

Year-ended April 5 . . . . *(insert year)*

We request a PAYE settlement agreement for the . . . . . *(insert year)* tax year onwards. We wish the agreement to cover liabilities arising on the following items:

. . . . *(insert details)*

. . . . *(insert details)*

. . . . *(insert details)*

The liabilities arising will be calculated on a grossed-up basis and by reference to the number of basic rate and higher rate taxpayers covered by the agreement.

The tax and Class 1B NI liability arising will be paid to the Collector of Taxes by October 19, following the end of each tax year.

We should be grateful if you would confirm your acceptance or otherwise of this before July 6 . . . . . . *(insert year)* in order that we may file form P11D in a timely manner.

Yours faithfully

. . . .*(insert name)*

Trivial benefits letter

If, following a PAYE visit, it's discovered that you've been giving away, say, Christmas gifts to your staff, but not recording them as benefits-in-kind on P11Ds, the Taxman may impose penalties and tax. What can you do to prevent this from happening?

SMALL GIFTS

The Taxman allows you to give small gifts to staff tax-free. The gift has to be "trivial" and cannot be money, something capable of being exchanged for money, or a voucher. The examples given in the Taxman's manual are items such as a turkey, a bottle of wine or a box of chocolates. The gift cannot be in reward for services as an employee. So a reward for the year's hard work will still attract tax whereas a seasonal goodwill gift will not. The total cost may be substantial where a large number of staff is involved, but provided the individual value of the gift remains trivial, no liability should arise - the number of employees has no bearing. As there's no clear definition of trivial, use the **Trivial Benefits Letter** to seek confirmation and agreement from the Taxman that the gifts concerned can by left off the P11Ds.

TRIVIAL BENEFITS LETTER

HMRC

.... *(insert address)*

....

....

....

.... *(insert date)*

Dear Sirs

.... ***(insert employer's PAYE reference)***

We intend to provide the following benefits to employees which we regard to be minor and trivial in nature .... *(insert description of benefit, number of staff to whom it is provided, unit cost and total cost to employer)*.

We should be grateful if you would confirm that these benefits would be regarded as trivial in nature and also confirm in writing that tax will not be sought and that details of the benefit need not be reported on the P11D/P9D.

(The following paragraph to be used in the event that benefits are covered by a PSA.)

We have provided the following benefits to employees and which are covered by a PAYE settlement agreement dated .... *(insert date of PSA)*.

.... *(insert description of benefit, number of staff to whom it is provided, unit cost and total cost to employer)*.

We should be grateful if you could confirm that these benefits will be regarded as trivial and confirm in writing that tax will not be sought. Please amend the PAYE settlement accordingly and confirm the amendment in writing.

Yours faithfully

.... *(insert signature)*

Homeworkers' expenses policy

The increasing tendency for individuals to work from home raises the question of which home-related costs can be reimbursed tax-free by an employer. So you'll need a company policy making it clear to your employees which expenses come with a tax bill.

WORKING FROM HOME

There has been a very large increase in the number of employees who work from home. A question often asked by employers is how the additional expenses the employee will incur as a result of working from home are to be met and what the correct tax treatment is for reimbursed expenses and the provision of equipment. The basic position is that if you provide an employee with equipment that can be used privately, there will be a benefits charge. It would be very difficult for you to keep a check on the use of the equipment and the Taxman should accept that the private use is insignificant as long as you have a clearly stated **Homeworkers' Expenses Policy** setting out when private use is accepted. In this case, there will be no tax or Class 1A NI due. The additional costs of such things as heating and lighting which arise due to working at home can be reimbursed without any charge to tax and NI.

HOMEWORKERS' EXPENSES POLICY

Provision of equipment

The Company will supply you with the necessary equipment that may reasonably be required to enable the contract to be performed from home. This may include some of the following:

- telephone
- fax machine
- laptop/desktop computer
- computer software/licences
- printer
- photocopier
- desk and chair
- filing cabinet(s)
- desk stationery
- writing materials.

An inventory will be kept as a means of recording the equipment supplied and you will be required to sign for the receipt of any equipment provided.

The equipment shall at all times remain the property of the Company, not be used for private purposes and be returned by you when you cease working from home. All equipment supplied by the Company will be covered under the Company's insurance policy.

Travel

You will be recorded as having your home as your permanent place of work. Therefore travel between your home and the Company's premises, or any other location visited on behalf of the Company, is regarded as business travel and will be reimbursed under the normal expenses policy rules.

Telephone

See the separate provision of home telephone policy.

Additional home expenses

The additional costs of such things as heating and lighting, which arise due to you working from home will be reimbursed at a flat rate of £3 per week.

Provision of home telephone policy

If you have an employee who works from home, you might think it's a good idea to have a landline installed there. What will the Taxman expect to find about this in your paperwork?

A CLEAR BUSINESS NEED

Where you pay directly for a telephone in your employee's home, they will have to pay tax and you'll have to pay employers' NI on the cost of the line rental and calls, less any amount reimbursed by the employee. However, if:

- you (the employer) are the subscriber

- there's a clear business need for the telephone

- you have procedures in place to ensure that private calls are kept to a minimum or that the employee reimburses you for the full cost of their private calls, then the employee won't be taxed on the line rental or the calls and you'll save the employers' NI.

Use our **Provision of Home Telephone Policy** to document your procedures.

PROVISION OF HOME TELEPHONE POLICY

If you are required to work from home on a regular basis, the Company will provide you with a separate telephone line for business use only.

The Company will contract directly with the telephone services provider.

You will reimburse the Company for the cost of any private calls made on a monthly basis at the actual cost (inclusive of VAT) as shown on the telephone services invoice.

Agreement

I agree to reimburse the Company for the actual cost of any private calls made using the separate business telephone line provided to me.

Signed . . . .

Dated . . . .

Mobile phone declaration

The old rule was that you could have as many mobile phones as you liked, tax and NI free. Now it's down to one per employee. If you have more than one, what can you do to minimise your tax bill?

CHOOSE YOUR EXEMPT PHONE

The tax exemption for employees who are provided with a mobile phone changed on April 6 2006. Directors/employees provided with more than one new phone by their company will need to consider which is to be the "exempt" phone and which the "taxable" phone. They can record this choice with a **Mobile Phone Declaration**. It will probably be for the phone they make most of their personal calls from. If the other phone is used strictly for business calls, then although in theory it's taxable, there is no tax bill because there are no private calls.

MOBILE PHONE DECLARATION

To: . . . . *(insert name of Company)*

I hereby elect that my new (post April 6 2006) company mobile phone (number . . . . *(insert mobile phone number))* shall be treated as my "exempt from tax" phone.

Signed . . . .

Date . . . .

Note.   *This declaration is only necessary if you have more than one mobile phone issued to you after April 6 2006.*

Assets with personal use

Where an asset is loaned to an employee there is usually a taxable benefit to declare. This document deals with assets (other than cars, vans, mobile phones and computers) owned by you as an employer but made available for private use by an employee.

RECORD YOUR ASSETS

Where an employee is provided with a company asset which they can use, either partly or completely, for a private purpose, e.g. a digital camera, its annual asset value needs to be reported on form P11D. For most assets, the annual value is 20% of market value when it was first provided to the employee. So in order for you to be able to calculate the amount to include on the P11D, use the **Assets with Personal Use** form and keep a print out of this as a record of the calculation. You will also need to record any amounts that the employee has reimbursed as these will reduce the benefit charge.

ASSETS WITH PERSONAL USE

Employee name: . . . .

Employee NI number: . . . .

Details of asset provided:

Description: . . . .

Original cost/market value: . . . .

Calculation of annual value:

	£	£
Greater of:		
(a) 20% of market value when first made available	1,000	
(b) rent or hire charges paid	0	
Annual value		1,000
Add: annual running costs (e.g. insurance)		100
		1,100
Less: amount made good by employee		0
Amount to enter on P11D		1,100

"Old" home computer benefit

Many employees are allowed to use a computer for private purposes even it's been supplied by the employer primarily for work purposes. Do you still have any computers provided before April 6 2006, which are worth less than £500? If so this document will help you calculate the benefit-in-kind figure under the old rules.

PROVIDED BEFORE APRIL 2006

The Home Computer Initiative was withdrawn in 2006, so for most computers held primarily for work purposes, there is potentially a benefit charge on their private use. If the annual value of the computer (including peripherals such as a printer) was less than £500 before April 6 2006, then there was no benefit charge. If you still have computers from before this date, use the **"Old" Home Computer Benefit** form to calculate whether you need to include a benefit on your employees' P11Ds.

For computers purchased after this date you should use the Electronic Devices Policy.

"OLD" HOME COMPUTER BENEFIT

Employee name: . . . .

Employee NI number: . . . .

Details of computer equipment provided:

Description:. . . . .

Original cost/market value: . . . .

Calculation of P11D value:

	£	£
Greater of:		
(a) 20% of market value when first made available	600	
(b) rent or hire charges paid	0	
Annual value		600
Add: annual running costs (e.g. insurance)		50
		650
Less: amount made good by employee		0
Less: computer exemption		500
Amount to enter on P11D		150

Electronic devices policy

In removing the Home Computer Initiative in 2006, the Taxman accidentally opened the door to charging tax on private use of any electronic device provided to employees by their company. How can you prevent a tax charge from arising?

COMPUTER-RELATED EQUIPMENT

The latest guidance from the Taxman is that the level of an employee's private usage of computer-related equipment provided by their company will not be the deciding factor in whether or not a tax charge arises. If it's made available in order to carry out their duties in the first place, then they are unlikely to be taxed on its private use. So to be able to prove this to the Taxman it's best to have an **Electronic Devices Policy** governing the issue (and private use) of each device.

ELECTRONIC DEVICES POLICY

1. Electronic devices are provided by . . . . *(insert company name)* to enable you to work efficiently and communicate effectively for business purposes.

2. Electronic devices are anything designed to be used, connected to, or inserted into a computer, including printers, scanners, modems, MP3 players and mobile phones with e-mail and Internet access e.g. BlackBerrys.

3. You must comply with the Company's e-mail and Internet policies at all times, and any breach of them will be regarded as a disciplinary matter.

4. The Company reserves the right to monitor your usage of electronic devices, e-mail and the Internet.

5. We have introduced this policy to ensure that:

    5.1.   you make efficient and proper use of IT and communications facilities

    5.2.   you do not put our computer systems at risk

    5.3.   we are protected from external intrusion

    5.4.   our image is properly protected

    5.5.   you are aware of what constitutes abuse of these facilities.

6. This policy will be reviewed and updated.

7. Reasonable use of the Company's e-mail facility for personal purposes is permitted. For more information on how the Company defines "reasonable" see . . . . . . *(insert contact name)*.

8. Reasonable use of the Company's Internet connection for personal purposes is permitted. For more information on how the Company defines "reasonable", see . . . . *(insert contact name)*.

9. You are responsible for the security of your electronic devices and must not allow them to be used by any unauthorised person. You should keep your passwords confidential and change them regularly. When leaving your computer unattended, or on leaving the office, you should make sure that you log off to prevent access in your absence.

Loan record

A taxable benefit may arise where a director or employee is provided with a loan, either interest-free or at a favourable rate of interest. Use this document to calculate what, if anything, you need to declare to the Taxman.

IMPORTANT TO MONITOR

Where a low-interest or interest-free loan is made to a P11D employee or director, a benefit-in-kind will have to be included if it's more than £5,000 at any time during the year. You can use the Taxman's P11D working sheet 4 to calculate the amount you need to include. However, it's important to monitor loans to ensure that they don't go over the £5,000 limit, so complete a **Loan Record** for all loans taken out by employees and directors.

LOAN RECORD

Record the date, description and amount the loan increases (+) or decreases (-) by.

For example:

Company name:		Employee's/Director's name:			
Subject: *Record of transactions going through the loan account*					
Date of transaction	Description of the transaction	Your initials	Loan increases ("+") £0.00	Loan decreases ("-") £0.00	Balance outstanding £0.00
January 1 2009	Opening balance	PJ	-	-	2,000.00
January 17 2009	Interest charged	PJ	100		2,100.00
January 28 2009	Amount repaid	PJ		(200)	1,900.00
February 2 2009	Further advance	PJ	500		2,400.00

Loan agreement

To avoid a payment to an employee/director being treated (and taxed) as additional salary, you could reclassify it as a fixed-rate loan. What documentation will the Taxman need to find to be convinced about this?

INEXPENSIVE FINANCE

The income tax paid by a director or employee on a subsidised loan provided by their employer is based on the difference between the interest rate actually charged and what is known as the "official rate". At present the official rate is 4.75%, subject to review in the event of significant changes. So a loan from your company remains a source of inexpensive, relatively short-term finance.

As evidence that the payments made to the employees should be treated as loans rather than salary, it's important to keep a copy of the **Loan Agreement**, setting out the terms of the loan and any interest that the employee has to pay.

LOAN AGREEMENT

THIS AGREEMENT is made on . . . . *(insert date)*

BETWEEN

(1) . . . . *(insert name of Lender)* of

. . . . *(insert address of Lender)* ("the Lender"); and

(2) . . . . *(insert name of Borrower)* of

. . . .*(insert address of Borrower)* (the "Borrower").

1. Amount of Loan

The Lender will lend to the Borrower and the Borrower will borrow from the Lender the sum of £. . . . . . *(insert amount)* "the Loan" on the terms which follow.

2. Interest

The Borrower shall pay to the Lender interest on the Loan at the rate of . . . . *(insert figure)* per annum quarterly on the last day of each of the months of [March June September and December] [January April July and October] [February May August and November] in each year. The first such payment to be made on whichever of the interest payment dates first occurs after the advance of the Loan and to be in respect of the period from and including the date of such advance until the next interest payment date.

3. Repayment

Unless otherwise agreed, the Borrower may only repay the Loan by a single payment on . . . . *(insert date)*.

4. Compulsory repayment subject to demand

The Lender may, by notice in writing to the Borrower, demand the immediate payment of all moneys due or incurred by the Borrower to the Lender together with all interest and any other sums forthwith (or otherwise as the Lender may require) at any time if the Borrower does not pay on the due date any money which may have become due hereunder or under any document supplemental hereto.

Chapter 4

Company cars and vans

Company cars and car allowances policy

Company cars are always at the top of the Taxman's hit list. Using our sample policy will help you to both dismiss his enquiries very quickly and avoid potentially sizeable tax bills and penalties.

WHY USE A POLICY?

If the provision of a company car or van is part of the employee's remuneration package, specific reference to this should be made in their contract of employment. The rule of thumb is that if a payment is part of the remuneration package then it is tax deductible for the company. This should be clear in your **Company Cars and Car Allowances Policy**. By including such a policy in your staff handbook, not only are you communicating your position to your employees, but you are also providing evidence to the Taxman that you only reimburse qualifying expenses.

COMPANY CARS AND CAR ALLOWANCES POLICY

Company cars

Subject to holding a current, full driving licence, some employees are provided with a car for use in the performance of their job duties. If you are provided with a company car, this will be set out in your contract of employment. Unless you are notified otherwise, a company car may be used for both business and private use, subject to such restrictions and upon such conditions (if any) as the Company may from time to time impose.

Employees are only provided with company cars at the discretion of the Company and it may change its rules and procedures on company cars at any time and from time to time.

The Company reserves the right to set a maximum lease value on company cars and/or to specify the make, model and colour that will be provided.

The Company will pay for the MOT, licensing, insurance, maintenance, repair and servicing of company cars (provided repairs and service are not caused by the employee's negligence or wilful default) and when necessary replacement thereof. However, employees have no contractual right to a replacement car. The Company will also pay for the cost of petrol/diesel (as appropriate) for business use only. The employee must pay for petrol/diesel for all private mileage.

The employee will be responsible for any income tax liability as assessed by the HMRC in respect of the use of the car.

The employee must not permit the car to be taken out of Great Britain without the prior consent of their manager.

The Company will retain all documents relating to the registration of the car. However, the employee is responsible for ensuring the car has a valid MOT certificate and a valid licence disc and for ensuring the car is properly maintained and serviced. As stated above, the Company will generally bear the cost of these matters.

The employee is also responsible for ensuring the car is properly looked after at all times and is responsible for the cleanliness of it, together with its equipment and fittings. The employee must ensure that it is kept in a roadworthy condition, that it conforms with current road traffic legislation and that the provisions and conditions of the policy of insurance relating thereto are observed and that such policy is not rendered void or voidable. The Company may seek to recoup any losses in the event of damage caused to the car by the employee's negligence or wilful default. In addition, the employee is responsible for the excess which is required to be paid which is not recoverable from the insurance company should the vehicle be involved in an accident, irrespective of liability for the accident. By signing their contract of employment, the employee accepts that the Company shall be entitled to deduct the cost of repair of any such damage and/or the cost of the insurance excess from the employee's wages.

Personal items are left in the car entirely at the employee's own risk and the Company does not accept any liability for loss, theft or damage of personal items.

The employee must report to the Company forthwith:

- vehicle defects
- any road traffic accident in which the employee may be involved whilst driving the car, whether or not it occurred on the Company business
- any fixed penalty notice or any order of any court to endorse the employee's driving licence or to disqualify them from holding a driving licence, whether or not that consequence occurred whilst driving on Company business
- any other event which results in the employee being ineligible to drive the car.

The employee is responsible for the payment of any and all fines incurred as a result of a motoring offence whilst the car is in the employee's possession, including parking and speeding fines and by signing their contract of employment the employee accepts that the Company shall be entitled to deduct the cost of any such fines from the employee's wages.

Upon request, the employee must provide their full driving licence for inspection.

Failure to observe these rules or failure to use the car in a reasonable and responsible manner may result in the Company withdrawing the use of the car from the employee concerned. In addition, a failure to observe these rules will be regarded as a disciplinary offence and will be dealt with in accordance with the Company's disciplinary procedure. Depending on the seriousness of the breach, it may constitute gross misconduct rendering the employee liable to summary dismissal.

On the termination of the employee's employment, or if they cease to hold a valid and current licence to drive private motor cars, the employee must promptly return or account for the car and deliver up the keys to . . . . *(insert name of contact)*. By signing the contract of employment, the employee accepts that failure to do so will entitle the Company to withhold any outstanding monies/wages due from the Company to the employee up to the value of the car.

Car allowances

In lieu of the provision of a company car, the employee may elect by notice in writing to the Company to receive a monthly car allowance of such amount as shall be notified by the Company from time to time. This allowance shall be added to and paid on the due date for payment of salary.

Driving and mobile phones

Some employees are required to drive on the Company's business as part of their job duties. Operating a mobile phone whilst driving reduces concentration and increases the likelihood of an accident. It is also a criminal offence. This section therefore also sets out the Company's requirements in relation to your using a mobile phone whilst driving on Company business. It applies irrespective of whether you use a Company-provided mobile phone or your own personal mobile phone and irrespective of whether you are driving a company car or your own car.

You are completely prohibited from using a hand-held mobile phone or similar hand-held electronic device whilst driving as part of your job duties, whether this is to make or receive telephone calls, send or read text or image/picture messages, send or receive facsimiles or to access the Internet or e-mail. If you are discovered contravening this rule, you will face serious action under the Company's disciplinary procedure. In view of the potential health and safety implications, it may also constitute gross misconduct and could render you liable to summary dismissal. If you do wish to use a hand-held mobile phone when driving, you must stop the car and completely turn off the car's engine before using it. A person is regarded as "driving" for the purposes of the law if the engine is running, even if their vehicle is stationary. This means you must not use a hand-held phone at traffic lights, in traffic jams or at other times when the engine is still running.

A hands-free phone is one that does not require you to hold it at any point during the course of its operation. A mobile phone that is attached to fixed speakers and does not require you to hold it whilst in use (e.g., because it is stored in a cradle) would be covered, as would a hands-free mobile phone with voice activation. If the phone needs to be held in your hand at some point during its operation, for example to dial the number or to end the call, it is not hands-free. If you are required to drive as part of your job duties and you wish to use your mobile phone, you must ensure you have the appropriate hands-free equipment for the phone. However, even with hands-free equipment, driving and conducting a telephone conversation are both demanding tasks and you should take all reasonable steps to ensure you do not carry out these tasks at the same time. You should therefore make use of any voicemail or call divert facility available, rather than make or receive "live" calls. You should then stop regularly in safe places to check for voicemail messages and to make and return calls. If you do need to make or receive a call whilst driving on Company business and you have the appropriate hands-free equipment, these calls should nevertheless be limited to essential calls and only when it is safe to do so.

Lump sum contribution agreement

Your employee wants a company car but you are not in a position to fund it completely. If the employee pays an amount towards its purchase price, this could cause complications with the Taxman. How can you set the record straight?

A capital contribution can be made by a director or employee towards the cost of either the car itself or any of the accessories which are taken into account in determining its price, for taxable benefit purposes. The Taxman may seek evidence that it was made around the time that the car or accessory was provided. There is a ceiling of £5,000 on the amount of any capital contribution which may be taken into account for these purposes.

Some tax inspectors have been known to take the view that payments made by an employee do not reduce the benefit charge. They are merely for the availability of a more expensive car. Not everybody would agree with this view but the Taxman is likely to defend it if challenged.

WHAT IF THE CAR IS SOLD?

Another problem with capital contributions comes when you cease to use the car (say, when you change it) and the money you've paid becomes refundable. The Taxman's line is that only a proportionate repayment is acceptable.

For example, if the car attracts a tax charge of 24% per year, then making a capital contribution of £5,000 will save you tax on £1,200 (£5,000 x 24%) p.a. If you are a higher rate taxpayer you save £480 p.a. (40% x £1,200).

So from a tax point of view it is helpful to have a **Lump Sum Contribution Agreement** in place where employees make a capital contribution to the purchase price of the vehicle.

LUMP SUM CONTRIBUTION AGREEMENT

Agreement concerning a capital contribution towards the purchase of company car registration . . . . *(insert registration number)* (the "Car") to be provided by . . . . *(insert company name)* (the "Company") for private use by . . . . . . *(insert name)* (the "Director/Employee").

The Employee agrees to make a capital contribution of . . . . *(insert figure*)* towards the purchase of the Car, to be paid by the employee within 30 days of the Car being purchased by the Company.

Upon sale of the Car, the Employee will be entitled to a refund of said capital contribution, but only after the Employee's share of depreciation in market value since purchase has been taken into account.

Agreement

As a condition of the Car being available, I agree to make the payment referred to above and accept a deduction for depreciation from any refund due to me when the Car is sold.

Signed . . . .

Date . . . .

* *maximum of £5,000.*

Top-up payments agreement

If an employee/director makes a monthly contribution towards the company car they really want, how can you make sure the Taxman reduces their tax bill accordingly?

STRUCTURING THE AGREEMENT

The Taxman's view is that an employee is allowed the use of a more expensive car if they pay a monthly sum representing, for example, the excess leasing cost. In this case, the payments by the employee would not reduce the benefit charge as they do not qualify as payments for the private use of the car. In the Taxman's view they are merely for the availability of a more expensive car. In practice, it is usually possible to structure an agreement to avoid this problem. Our **Top-up Payments Agreement** has this purpose in mind although it would make sense to obtain written approval from the company's PAYE office confirming that the wording will achieve the desired effect.

TOP-UP PAYMENTS AGREEMENT

Agreement concerning use of the company car registration . . . . *(insert registration number)* (the "Car") provided by . . . . *(insert company name)* (the "Company") for private use by . . . . *(insert name)* (the "Director/Employee").

Until further notice, the Company is making the Car available to the Employee for his private use, subject to the Employee making a payment to the Company for that private use. The payment will be . . . . *(insert figure*)* or such other amount as the Company may, in its discretion, advise in writing and will be deducted from the Employee's net monthly pay.

As a condition of the Car being available for private use, I agree to make the payment referred to above for that use.

Signed . . . .

Date . . . .

*   *This could be either a fixed amount or an amount calculated by a formula. The following are examples of the wording that could be used:*

(a) *£100; or*

(b) *the figure calculated as 20% of the leasing cost of the car for the previous month, or*

(c) *the figure calculated as 20p per private mile in excess of 750 private miles driven in the previous month.*

Business mileage record

The Taxman will expect you to keep a record of the amounts paid for business mileage and the business journeys to which they relate.

OWN CAR

Under the Approved Mileage Allowance Payments Scheme (AMAPS), the Taxman allows employees using their own cars for business journeys to claim a fixed-rate per mile, currently 40p per mile for the first 10,000 miles and 25p per mile after that.

Provided payments made to employees are not more than the AMAPS, no benefit-in-kind needs to be reported on P11Ds and nor are they reported in any other way. However, the Taxman would expect that every journey is identifiable from your records, not just a total monthly mileage amount.

One way of doing this is by getting employees to fill out a monthly **Business Mileage Record** in addition to their expense claim. The tax-free rates do not change depending on the number of miles driven in a tax year so that's one less thing to monitor with company car drivers.

COMPANY CARS

Since the introduction of the CO_2 emissions regime in 2002, there hasn't been the need to keep a record of all the business miles company car drivers cover. However, the Taxman will expect you to keep a record of the amounts paid for business mileage and the business journeys they are for.

Our record includes the current advisory fuel rates for the cost of the fuel for business journeys.

BUSINESS MILEAGE RECORD

Name . . . . Car registration . . . .

Business journeys during the month of . . . .   Year . . . .

Date	From	To	Reason	Miles	Claim £

Notes

HMRC expects the Company to keep a record of the amounts paid for business mileage in your company car and the business journeys they are for. To facilitate this you are required to fill out a monthly mileage record in addition to your normal expense claim for business miles travelled at the "advisory fuel rates for company cars".

Current advisory fuel rates for company cars are:

Engine size	Rate per mile		
	Petrol	Diesel	LPG
Less than 1,400cc	10p	10p	7p
1,401cc - 2,000cc	12p	10p	8p
Over 2,000cc	18p	13p	12p

Private fuel agreement

If an employer pays for even £1 of fuel for a private journey in a company car, the full tax charge for car fuel hits. What do you need to have in place to escape this charge?

No tax charge

To avoid a taxable benefit arising on fuel provided for private journeys in a company car (car fuel benefit), the employee should pay for all the fuel and then claim a fuel-only rate for the business miles they drive. The Taxman accepts that if the rate per mile is no more than a certain amount there's no tax charge for the employee and the employer won't have to pay NI on it either. No benefit-in-kind will need to be reported on the P11D and they do not need to be included in a dispensation.

Cover yourself

But if a mistake occurs and you inadvertently pay for any element of a private journey the full tax charge hits. To escape the charge in these circumstances you'll need to have in place a **Private Fuel Agreement** under which the employee is required to reimburse the entire cost of private fuel.

PRIVATE FUEL AGREEMENT

Agreement concerning fuel for use in company car . . . . *(insert registration number)* provided by the Company for . . . . *(insert name of the director/employee)*.

The Company will pay for the cost of petrol/diesel (as appropriate) for business use of your company car. You will pay for petrol/diesel for all private mileage.

If the Company inadvertently pays for petrol/diesel for your private mileage during a tax year (April 6 to April 5) you will reimburse the Company for this (at HMRC's fuel only rate per mile).

For example, the Company pays you for the cost of fuel for a journey, which later turns out in fact not to have been genuine business mileage. You are then required to make good the cost of that fuel.

Ideally this payment will be made within the tax year but must be made without unreasonable delay.

Agreement

I agree to make the payment referred to above if the Company inadvertently pays for my private fuel.

Signed . . . .

Date . . . .

Memo: invoices for motor expenses

How expenses are controlled is always at the top of the Taxman's list of questions during a compliance visit. Using our memo should help you to dismiss his enquiries about motor expenses very quickly, before they become too detailed.

COMPLIANCE VISIT

A compliance visit is often referred to as a PAYE visit, i.e. an inspection of your books and records centred around your payroll but specifically trying to unearth, as yet, untaxed payments and benefits-in-kind. The inspectors will ask for a full list of the current balances on your nominal ledger, and then for an analysis of what has been posted to accounts, such as cleaning, repairs, motor expenses, entertainment etc. They are looking for hidden payments to, or benefits for, employees. This is where having a computerised accounts system can come in handy and you can simply print out what's in there. They will also trust you to go and get any invoices they are interested in looking at.

COVER YOURSELF

As a rule of thumb, every invoice relating to a company car needs to be in the name of the employer for it to get a tax deduction for the expense. It will save problems later if you make this problem clear to employees, you can use our **Memo: Invoices for Motor Expenses**. Following this up with a review of all motor expenses invoices over, say, £300 should limit your exposure to this sort of error. If you do find a mistake send a copy of the invoice back to the supplier and ask for one in the company's name.

MEMO: INVOICES FOR MOTOR EXPENSES

To: all employees with company cars

It has come to the Company's attention that certain motor expenses claims have been submitted without the appropriate documentation being attached. In order for the company to recover these costs for tax purposes and to avoid company car drivers being taxed on a separate benefit-in-kind please take note that:

1. Invoices for repairs and maintenance

The Company will pay for the MOT, licensing, insurance, maintenance, repair and servicing of company cars. However, the contract/invoice for said maintenance, repair and servicing **must** be in the name of the Company, not the company car driver.

2. Accessories

If a vehicle is used for business purposes, VAT on repairs and maintenance can be recovered provided the work done is paid for by the Company. However, VAT charged on accessories fitted to a car when it is purchased cannot be reclaimed even if separately itemised on the sales invoice. VAT can be reclaimed on accessories subsequently purchased and fitted to a vehicle for business reasons, provided the accessory remains part of the vehicle.

. . . . *(insert signature of MD or FD)*

. . . . *(insert date)*

Use of van agreement

If your company makes a van available for your private use then there is a benefit-in-kind. This charge comes into play when private use exceeds normal business commuting.

Avoid private use

There is a fixed taxable benefit charge of £3,000 a year for private use of a van (with a laden weight of 3.5 tonnes or less). This charge comes into play when private use exceeds normal commuting.

You should make it a condition of the driver's employment that whilst they can use the van for ordinary commuting, no other private use (i.e. any non-business journey excluding commuting) is permitted by them (or their family) unless they pay for it.

The Taxman is likely to accept that the van is only used for ordinary commuting if the employee has the use of an alternative vehicle for private journeys. If they have no other access to a vehicle, the Taxman may question the private use; so make a note of the situation in your records. "Insignificant" use is permitted without triggering a scale charge, for example, using the van in an emergency or for an occasional short journey. If any of your drivers fit into the insignificant private use category there should be no charge and nothing to declare on your employers' annual return of benefits and expenses for the tax year.

We've included a **Use of Van Agreement** banning private use which should enable you to avoid the charge altogether.

USE OF VAN AGREEMENT

Agreement concerning use of company van registration . . . . *(insert registration number)* (the "Van") provided by . . . . *(insert company name)* (the "Company") to . . . . *(insert name)* (the "Director"/"Employee"), NI number . . . . *(insert NI number)*.

The Van is made available to the Employee for travel on Company business. The Employee is permitted to use the Van for ordinary commuting to and from home, the Employee's place of work, but all other private use is strictly prohibited. According to the HMRC guidance, prohibited private use includes using the van to do the supermarket shopping each week, taking the van away on a week's holiday or using the van outside of work for social activities.

The Employee is also required to keep a daily mileage log in the vehicle recording the reason for the journey and the number of business miles travelled.

Agreement

As a condition of the Van being provided to me, I confirm that it will not be used for any private purpose except ordinary commuting between my home and place of work.

Signed . . . .

Date . . . .

Pool car status letter

A pool car can be very tax efficient but in order to get one past the Taxman you'll need to meet his conditions. There must be no private use of the vehicle and a record must be kept of journeys. Compile all your evidence and send to the Taxman for approval.

NO PRIVATE USE

Get a pool car past the Taxman and you can secure some excellent tax savings - no taxable benefit on the driver, no fuel benefit charge and no employers' NI. To obtain this status you'll need to gather evidence together about the use of the pool car.

The conditions that have to be met are: **(1)** it must be available to and be used by more than one employee; **(2)** it must not be used by one employee to the exclusion of others; **(3)** it should not normally be kept overnight at an employee's home; and **(4)** it must not be used for private journeys except as a small part of a business journey. Given that the rules provide a total exemption from any tax charge, it's not surprising that the Taxman applies them very strictly.

CONFIRMATION

Use our **Pool Car Status Letter** to work through what the Taxman is after. Send it in with copies of the employees' driving licences and the Pool Car Journey Record. The decision about whether the vehicle will be accepted as a pool car will normally be taken by a local (district) level inspector, although an appeal may be made on the issue to the Commissioners.

POOL CAR STATUS LETTER

. . . . *(insert name)*

HMRC

. . . . *(insert address)*

Your ref: . . . .*(insert employer's PAYE reference)*

. . . . *(insert date)*

Dear . . . . *(insert name)*

RE: Pool Car Status

The purpose of this letter is to seek confirmation that we are correctly treating certain company vehicles as pool cars. In support of this assertion we make the following points and have enclosed supporting evidence.

The car is available to and used by more than one employee

Naturally everyone who needs to make business trips uses the vehicle(s). Attached are:

(1) Photocopies of driving licences of all the employee drivers.

(2) A copy of a journey record for the month of . . . . . . *(insert month)* for each pool car, this representative period clearly shows that the vehicles in question are used by more than one employee.

(3) Copies of letters to the Company's insurance broker notifying them of the people using the vehicle, plus their reply notifying us of the increase in premium.

Any private use is incidental to its business use

There is of course a de minimus private use with any pool vehicle but ours is small in extent and infrequent representing as it does, on average, no more than 5% of the vehicle's annual mileage. For example, an employee staying away from home overnight because of a business trip may use the car to go out for a meal in the evening, because this is merely incidental to the main business journey.

Kept overnight on the business premises

Occasionally an employee takes a car home so as to make an early start on a business journey the following morning. It is company policy to allow this only where starting the journey form the company's premises would have caused unreasonable delay. A copy of the company Pool Car Policy is attached.

The total number of nights on which the pool car was taken home for any reason in the (representative period studied by the Company) was [. . . . . *(insert percentage)* %] which is a lot less than the 60% nights of the year (or period) rule of thumb we understand you normally accept.

Yours sincerely

. . . . *(insert signature)*

Pool car policy

Banning private use is essential for it to be considered a pool car by the Taxman. A verbal ban may work but it is far more sensible to have a policy written into the employee's contract. This will also help convince an inspector that you operate a genuine pool car arrangement.

TERMS OF USE

Verbally banning employees from using pool cars for private journeys was good enough for one VAT tribunal; however, we recommend that you'll be on much safer ground by introducing a **Pool Car Policy**. Always make your intentions clear from the start of a pool car arrangement by explicitly banning private journeys. This way when buying your next pool car you should be able to claim back the VAT on it.

This policy lays out the terms of use for pool cars: that private use is banned, all journeys are to be logged on the pool car journey record, and that the car should not be kept at someone's house except in exceptional circumstances.

The policy also makes it clear that each car is not for the exclusive use of one particular person, this is vitally important for establishing its pool car status. The car must be driven only by authorised personnel and you must obtain a copy of their driving licence before you allow them to drive the car. All fuel must be paid for by the company.

There is also a clause relating to damage to the vehicle. By signing the employment contract the employee is agreeing to repay the company should the car be damaged due to the employee's negligence or wilful neglect. They will also accept responsibility for an excess payment should the car be involved in an accident, regardless of the circumstances.

Together with the journey record, by including this policy in your employee's contract it should help to convince an inspector that you operate a genuine pool car arrangement.

POOL CAR POLICY

A pool car can be made available (but not exclusively) to some employees for use in the performance of their job duties subject to them holding a current, full driving licence. A pool car must only be used for business journeys, the car must be kept overnight at the Company's premises, and is subject to any other such restrictions and upon such conditions (if any) as the Company may from time to time impose. In particular, only authorised employees can drive the pool car. Under no circumstances may any other person drive the car. The cost of petrol/diesel (as appropriate) in running the pool car is paid for by the Company.

Employees are only provided with a pool car at the discretion of the Company and it may change its rules and procedures on pool cars at any time and from time to time.

If, occasionally, an employee takes a car home so as to make an early start on a business journey the following morning, it is Company policy to allow this only where starting the journey form the company's premises would have caused unreasonable delay

An employee staying away from home overnight because of a business trip may use the car to go out for a meal in the evening.

The Company may seek to recoup any losses in the event of damage caused to the car by the employee's negligence or wilful neglect. In addition, the employee is responsible for the excess which is required to be paid which is not recoverable from the insurance company should the vehicle be involved in an accident, irrespective of the responsibility for the accident. By signing their contract of employment, the employee accepts that the Company shall be entitled to deduct the cost of repair of any such damage and/or the cost of the insurance excess from the employee's wages.

Personal items are left in the car entirely at the employee's own risk and the Company does not accept any liability for loss, theft or damage of personal items.

The employee must report to the Company forthwith: vehicle defects, any road traffic accident, any fixed penalty notice or any order of any court to endorse the employee's driving licence or to disqualify them from holding a driving licence, whether or not that consequence occurred whilst driving on Company business, and any other event which results in the employee being ineligible to drive the car.

Upon request, the employee must provide their full driving licence for inspection.

Failure to observe these rules will be regarded as a disciplinary offence and will be dealt with in accordance with the Company's disciplinary procedure. Depending on the seriousness of the breach, it may constitute gross misconduct rendering the employee liable to summary dismissal.

Pool car journey record

In order to apply for pool car status you will need to provide evidence of how the car is used. The Taxman will expect you to keep a record of all the journeys undertaken to show that they were for business purposes. When you apply for pool car status you will need to include this record.

PROOF OF JOURNEY

To satisfy the Taxman that a vehicle is a genuine pool car, there are several steps which must be taken. Using our **Pool Car Journey Record** is an excellent way of proving who uses the car, why it has been used and when the journey took place.

This will provide proof that there has been no private use of the vehicle (except for the rare the occasion when it forms part of a business journey; for example, to keep an early appointment, the employee takes the car home the night before).

Keep the record in the glove compartment of the car for the duration of the month, so there can be no excuses about failure to complete it. However, do ensure that the form is filed away at the end of the month. Make sure the records are kept safely; even after pool car status is confirmed it will be checked by an inspector every three or four years.

POOL CAR JOURNEY RECORD

For the month of . . . .   *(insert month)*

Pool car . . . .   *(insert make, model and registration of car)*

Driver	Date	Journey(s)		Notes
		From	**To**	

Chapter 5

Status

Checklist of status factors

Self-employed workers can be a ticking tax bomb. If the Taxman decides they should have been treated as your employees, he will ask for the PAYE and NI you should have deducted from their wages plus the employers' NI due. This tax bill can cover up to six tax years if the self-employed workers have been working for you throughout this period. So how can you prove their employee status?

EMPLOYED OR SELF-EMPLOYED?

Ideally, you'd want all your workers to be self-employed - then you could avoid paying employers' NI, holiday and sick pay, etc. Unfortunately, you're not free to choose and the Taxman is increasingly looking to challenge the status of self-employed workers and reclassify them as employed. Get it wrong and you, not the worker, will be liable for the unpaid tax and NI.

Deciding whether a worker is employed or self-employed isn't easy. And it's not helped by the fact that neither employment nor self-employment are defined in the legislation. However, there have been many cases concerning employment status and the message from these is that there are several factors to take into consideration. Our **Checklist of Status Factors** lists the most important. Fill it out as part of your procedure for taking on a new worker. Keep it as evidence to show the Taxman the reasons why you treated them as self-employed. Case law shows that it is not necessary to answer "yes" to all of the questions in order to demonstrate self-employed status. You may only need one really strong indicator of self-employment to put the business into quite a safe position. Failing this, a number of weaker pointers towards self-employment coupled with the absence of any strong points against, should equally put you in a safe position. The main thing to bear in mind if ever faced by a status enquiry from the Taxman is that he isn't the sole arbiter of determining employment status and his view can certainly be challenged.

CHECKLIST OF STATUS FACTORS

Worker's name and trading as name: . . . .

NI number: . . . .

	Y	N
Strong indicators:		
• Would you allow the worker to provide a substitute if necessary, payment of whom will be their responsibility?	❏	❏
• You are not obliged to provide the worker with work e.g. during slow periods?	❏	❏
• Can the worker turn down work?	❏	❏
• Does the worker also work for other contractors?	❏	❏
• Does the worker provide their own tools and equipment which are fundamental to the work being carried out? (Small hand tools would be a weaker indicator.)	❏	❏
• Does the worker have to put right any errors or supply replacement materials at their own expense?	❏	❏
• No company or employee benefits are provided to the worker including paid holidays, sick pay or redundancy entitlement?	❏	❏
• Does the worker provide their own indemnity cover?	❏	❏
Weak indicators:		
• Does the contract specify that it is a contract for services?	❏	❏
• Is the basis of remuneration a fixed fee for work done rather than a rate per hour?	❏	❏
• Does the worker have headed notepaper and invoices and bill the company for work regularly done?	❏	❏
• Is the worker free to work their own hours?	❏	❏
• Does the worker have control over how the work is done?	❏	❏
• Is it clear to the other company workers that the individual concerned is a contract worker and self-employed?	❏	❏
• Can you only terminate the agreement for a serious breach of contract?	❏	❏

A "Yes" answer is indicative of self-employment while a "No" answer indicates employment.

Decision (Self-employed or employed?): . . . .

Made by: . . . .

Contract for services

The Taxman's aim is to reclassify freelancers such as consultants as employees and insist that PAYE and NI is due on the total amount paid to them. What evidence can you provide to avoid this particular bill?

TAKING ON INDEPENDENT CONTRACTORS

The Taxman is normally looking for expenses that you've claimed for in arriving at your taxable profit, which he thinks you shouldn't get a tax deduction for. However, his current focus during a compliance visit appears to be freelancers, payments to whom might not be apparent from a review of your accounts.

CONTRACTS FOR SERVICES

Contracts *for* services need to be distinguished from contracts *of* service (i.e. of employment). Under a **Contract for Services** you can only order what is to be done, while in the case of an employee under a contract of service, not only can you say what is to be done, but also how it is to be done. Arguably the most important element in a contract for services is a substitution clause. This allows the contractor to send in another suitably qualified worker in their place. Four points should be borne in mind when setting up a contract with an independent contractor:

- the right of substitution should not be limited to situations where the named worker is unable to work
- you should not be given the right to veto substitutes unless they are not suitably qualified
- you should not be able to arrange for the substitute
- the payment to the substitute must be the responsibility of the contractor and not your company.

A REALISTIC CONTRACT

Have a realistic contract between you and any freelancers you use. Ensure that your contract with them: **(1)** does not include phrases that give the impression that they are under the company's control; **(2)** gives no certainty of continuing work (this means that the Taxman cannot contend what is termed "mutuality of obligation"); **(3)** includes a substitution clause; and **(4)** does not give them any employee rights such as holiday or sick pay, pension rights etc. Make sure that reality matches contract; for example, check that they are not listed in the internal telephone list of employees, and don't have the right to attend staff events (other than as an invited guest). They might even have a different security pass compared to employees.

CONTRACT FOR SERVICES

1. The Company has agreed to enter into a contract for services with *(insert name of contractor)*. This agreement will commence on . . . . *(insert date)* and is scheduled to terminate on . . . . *(insert date)*. Details of the work to be undertaken can be found on the attached schedule *(insert this where appropriate)*.

2. . . . . *(insert name of contractor)* may offer a substitute contractor in their place, providing that all the following conditions are met:

   • the services provided by the proposed substitute remain as detailed above

   • the Company is satisfied that any substitute is suitable. In practice, this will mean that he possesses the necessary qualifications and experience to fulfil the terms of the contract

   • the Company is satisfied that the proposed substitute has sufficient resources to perform the contract to a sufficiently high standard

   • the Company is satisfied that the intended substitute will comply with its rules on confidentiality, health, safety and security

   • the costs associated with any training of the substitute and handover period will be met by . . . . *(insert name of contractor)*.

Consent to the proposed substitution is given to . . . . *(insert name of contractor)* in writing first.

The Company reserves the right to refuse a proposed substitute only if the substitute does not have the necessary skills and cannot fulfil the contractual requirements.

3. . . . . *(insert name of contractor)* agrees that this contract does not confer an employer/employee relationship between the parties at any time.

Name . . . .   Name . . . .

(insert name of contractor)   *(insert name of Company representative)*

                                                                 Name . . . .

                                                                 (insert name of Company)

Signed . . . .   Signed . . . .

Dated . . . .   Dated . . . .

Exchange of letters

During routine compliance visits the Taxman has been asking companies for the names and addresses of any freelancers they use. Protect yourself with an exchange of letters between your company and the freelancer.

PROVING YOU'VE CONSIDERED STATUS

The Taxman would be delighted to be able to reclassify your consultants/freelancers as your employees, as he could then insist that PAYE and NI is due on the total amount paid to them. One way to prevent this problem is to implement an **Exchange of Letters** with the freelancer on the practical aspects of their independence. This proves you have both have seriously considered this assignment and genuinely regard the freelancer as independent and not an employee. Your letter and the reply from the contractor should include references to the fact that: **(1)** they have an office at home; **(2)** they bring their personal laptop computer in to the office when they do work for you; **(3)** they have a desktop at home that they use for their other clients; **(4)** they hold business insurance; **(5)** they have a business identity (business stationery, business cards and company-headed invoices); and **(6)** they have a company business bank account through which you intend to settle their invoices.

EXCHANGE OF LETTERS

1. Letter from Company to freelancer

(For example, from ABC Software Ltd to Keith Wilson)

. . . . *(insert date)*

Dear . . . . *(insert name of freelancer, e.g. Keith)*

This letter is to confirm the points raised in the legal contract for services that both the Company and you have signed, and also deals with certain other subsidiary matters.

You have signed a contract for services, and your role with the Company from . . . . *(insert date, e.g. May 1 2009)* will be as a self-employed computer consultant. Additional practical points are:

1. Your title will be . . . . *(insert title, e.g. independent software consultant)*.

2. Although we shall expect you to work with . . . . *(insert name, e.g. senior software manager, Brian Dennis)*, your relationship with them will be one of mutual co-operation, rather than your being under their management and control.

3. Your name will not be included in the internal telephone list, as you are not an employee of the Company.

4. You will be issued with a special pass for contractors and sub-contractors, enabling you to gain access to the Company's premises.

5. Although you will have access to the Company restaurant and be able to purchase lunch etc., you will not be able to use the facilities of the Company sports and health club. Attendance at any staff functions will be by invitation only as a guest.

6. Your working hours are to be agreed between you and . . . . *(insert name)*. You will not be expected to "clock in" and "clock out".

7. You should present your monthly invoice to . . . . *(insert name)* at the end of each month. The Company guarantees to make payment to you by . . . . . *(insert date)* of the following month.

8. You are not eligible for sick pay or pension contributions.

9. The Company will not pay holiday pay or Bank Holiday pay. Once again, it is up to you to make mutually convenient arrangements with . . . . *(insert name)* when you intend to be away.

10. You are responsible for payment of your own income tax and NI contributions.

11. The Company expects you to arrange your own business insurance cover.

12. When it is necessary for personnel outside the company to be contacted in connection with your work, you should make clear that you are a consultant, or arrange for an appropriate employee to deal with the matter on your behalf.

13. As set out in this contract, the Company will make payment to you for hours worked at the rate agreed.

14. When you are not available, and it is necessary for someone else to cover for you, we understand that your colleague . . . . *(insert name)* will substitute for you.

15. This contract is for a fixed period. If, at a later date, we would like to retain you for a further period, we will negotiate accordingly. There is no certainty that future work will be available.

We look forward to seeing you on . . . . *(insert date, e.g. May 1).*

Yours sincerely

. . . . *(insert name)*

Director

2. Response from freelancer to Company

. . . . *(insert date)*

Dear   *(insert name of a director of the company)*

Thank you for your recent letter, and I note the points raised. I would add the following:

1. I reserve the right to complete work for other clients in addition to my work for . . . . *(insert name of company, e.g. ABC Software Ltd).*

2. Although I shall be using . . . . *(insert name of Company)*'s software and hardware, I shall arrange to bring my own laptop computer into the office. I have a desktop computer at home that I use for my other clients.

3. I shall be retaining my office at home, and expect to do a certain amount of work for . . . . *(insert name of Company)* there.

4. I confirm that I hold public liability and other business insurance.

5. My monthly invoices will be submitted on headed paper.

6. I have business cards printed that identify me as an independent contractor.

7. I have a business bank account, and would like my fees to be paid by electronic means into this account. I will arrange for you to have the necessary account details.

I look forward to a successful and rewarding business relationship with the Company.

Yours sincerely

. . . . *(insert signature)*

. . . . *(insert name)*

IR35 calculator

**IR35 potentially affects any consultant who,
rather than working under a direct employment contract with a
customer, contracts their services through a one-man company.
If you are likely to be caught by the IR35 legislation, how much this
will cost you in tax?**

PERSONAL SERVICE COMPANY

In April 2000, a new tax rule came into force (known as IR35), which potentially affects any consultant who, rather than working under a direct employment contract with a customer, contracts their services through a one-man or "personal service" company. By taking dividends rather than being paid a salary, the consultant can make substantial tax savings. The test for IR35 is whether, ignoring the existence of the company, the contract as it operates between the customer and the consultant is one which would lead to the consultant being classified as an employee of the customer, rather than self-employed. If the answer is "yes", the consultant would indeed be classified as an employee and IR35 applies. If they would be classified as self-employed, it does not. If IR35 applies, then the consultant would be required to pay tax as if they were an employee.

Effectively, tax on 95% of turnover is charged, with a deduction only for employee-allowed expenses and professional indemnity insurance. Use our **IR35 Calculator** to work out the potential liability. **Note.** The extra tax is a liability of the consultant company and not the customer company.

IR35 CALCULATOR

Company: . . . .   *(insert company name)*

Year end: . . . .   *(insert year end)*

	£	£
Turnover in tax year		
Less: 5% for expenses		
Add: Payments/benefits rec'd from Client		
Less: **Allowable expense items**		
Business motor expenses		
Business travel		
Professional subscriptions		
Capital allowances		
Entertaining		
Other expenses		
Necessary protective clothing		
Flat rate expenses		
Less: Employers' pension payments		
Employers' NI on actual pay		
Less: Actual pay and BIK's		
Deemed pay (inc Ers' NI)		
Ers' NI on above (12.8% of 112.8%)		
Deemed Pay (liable to PAYE/NI)		
Tax & NI on deemed remuneration		
Deemed pay (see above)		0
Personal allowance (if applicable)		6,475.00
Taxable Income		
Tax @ 20% on		
Tax @ 40% on		
Total tax due		
Ees' NI		
Ers' NI		
Total tax & NI due		

Consultancy agreement

Evidence in a status enquiry comes from many sources. However, as a minimum you'll need a realistic consultancy agreement between you and any freelancers you use.

INSPECTORS ON THE LOOKOUT

Ideally, if you want to take on an extra pair of hands to cope with a busy period, you would want them to be a self-employed independent contractor; then you could avoid paying employers' NI, holiday and sick pay etc. But unfortunately, simply hiring someone who claims to be self-employed isn't enough, and PAYE inspectors are always on the lookout for gross payments made by the business to individuals who, although they submit invoices, are effectively employed and not self-employed.

BE ON THE SAFE SIDE

If you want to take on a contractor on a fixed-term contract, e.g. for three months, only deal with people working through a limited company, and make sure that the contract is with it and not the contractor personally. Where appropriate, re-write your contracts using our **Consultancy Agreement** as a basis.

It may seem obvious but make sure that all contractors sign the agreement together with their contract for services before they commence work.

CONSULTANCY AGREEMENT

THIS AGREEMENT is dated . . . . *(insert date)*

Between

. . . . ("the Client"); and

. . . . ("the Supplier") *(insert your company name)*.

IT IS AGREED as follows:

1. The Supplier's services

The Supplier undertakes to supply the following services as follows: *(insert details)*

. . . .

The terms of this Agreement will apply to all Services provided by the Supplier to the Client during the currency of this Agreement. However, the Client is not obliged to provide the Supplier with a minimum or any number of orders over a period of time.

2. Duration

The Agreement will be deemed to have commenced on . . . . *(insert date)* and will continue until terminated in accordance with clause 9 or by mutual consent.

3. Performance of the services

The Supplier will be solely responsible for determining all matters of detail as to the manner in which the Services are performed, and for ensuring that all work done is of an objectively acceptable quality.

4. Independent contractor status

4.1. The Supplier is engaged as an independent contractor. Nothing herein will be deemed or construed to create a joint venture, partnership, agency or employee/employer relationship for any purpose.

4.2. The Supplier is solely responsible for payment of all taxes and NI contributions in respect of their fees and the Supplier hereby indemnifies the Client in respect of any claims that may be made by the relevant authorities against the Client in respect of income tax or NI or similar contributions relating to the Supplier's services.

5. Fee

The fee for the work shall be £ . . . . *(insert amount)*, which shall be exclusive of VAT (if applicable).

At the conclusion of the work (or at such intermediate stages as may be specified in the contract details), the Supplier will render an invoice for the fee on headed notepaper.

6. Provision of equipment

The Supplier will undertake the Services substantially using their own equipment and materials, the costs of which shall be deemed to have been included within the fee. Any equipment provided by the Client will be minor in scale and nature relative to this Agreement and the Client will be entitled to be reimbursed its reasonable costs of providing them.

7. Suitably qualified person

7.1.   The Supplier will provide a suitably qualified person to carry out the work.

7.2.   This person may be substituted by another suitably qualified person at the Supplier's expense. If the substitute does not have the necessary skills and cannot fulfil the contractual requirements then the Client reserves the right to terminate the contract.

7.3.   The costs associated with any handover period will be met by the Supplier.

8. Insurance

The Supplier shall be responsible for arranging (and meeting the cost of) such insurance as they think fit in connection with this Agreement. The Client's insurance policies do not apply to any work carried out under this agreement, except to the limited extent that they would in any event protect members of the general public.

9. Termination

If the Supplier fails to perform any of the Services to the reasonable satisfaction of the Client and such failure is capable of remedy, then the Client shall instruct the Supplier to perform the work and the Supplier shall at its own cost and expense remedy such failure (and any damage resulting from such failure) within 14 days or such other period of time as the Client may direct.

In the event that the Supplier fails to comply with this clause, the Client reserves the right to terminate the Agreement by notice in writing with immediate effect.

10. English law shall apply to this Agreement

Signed by or on behalf of the Client . . . . *(insert name)*

Signed by or on behalf of the Supplier . . . . *(insert name)*

Chapter 6

VAT

Invoice checklist

From time to time the VATman makes a fuss about invoices complying with new EU regulations. So what's the problem with the ones you've got? Do you need to ditch your invoices and start from scratch?

Valid VAT invoices

If you're registered for VAT, you can generally offset any VAT your suppliers have charged you (input VAT) against any VAT you charge your customers (output VAT). This offset is made by you putting a figure in the inputs box on your VAT return. This self-declaration method is on the condition that you keep specific evidence to back it up. The regulations look for a "valid tax invoice" and stipulate exactly what information has to appear on it.

Usually the changes are only tinkering and the chances are that you comply already. Even if you do get it wrong the system requires a warning to be issued for a first offence. If you ignore that then, yes, there is a small fine.

However, a VAT inspector will have certain things he wishes to look at. On the input VAT side he's likely to ask for copies of invoices over £1,000 for vetting against his own checklist. So we've provided a useful **Invoice Checklist** for scrutinising supplier invoices. To manage your own risk, check a sample of invoices, say, those over £1,000 (depending on quantity) each quarter. Failures are returned to the supplier for correction.

You can also use our checklist to vet your own sales invoices to see if they pass the VATman's test.

INVOICE CHECKLIST

Where tax is reclaimed in respect of a supply received from a registered trader, you are required to hold a valid tax invoice from that supplier. So does the invoice you are checking have:

1. An identifying number?

2. The date of the supply and the date when the invoice was issued?

3. The name, address and VAT registration number of the supplier?

4. Your name and address (i.e. the person to whom the goods or services were supplied)?

5. The type of supply by reference to the following categories:

   a) a supply by sale

   b) a supply on hire purchase or any similar transaction

   c) a supply by loan

   d) a supply by way of exchange

   e) a supply on hire, lease or rental

   f) a supply of goods made from customers' materials

   g) a supply by sale on commission

   h) a supply by sale or return or similar terms

   i) any other type of supply which the Commissioners may at any time by notice specify?

6. A description sufficient to identify the goods or services supplied?

7. For each description, the quantity of the goods or the extent of the services, the rate of tax and the amount payable (excluding tax)?

8. The total amount payable (excluding tax)?

9. The rate of any cash discount offered?

10. The amount of tax chargeable at each VAT rate, with the rate to which it relates and

11. The total amount of tax chargeable?

Note: The amounts need to be expressed in Sterling.

Warning! If any of the above information is missing from the document, it is not a valid tax invoice and you have no legal entitlement to reclaim the tax on it. It is not unknown for an input tax claim to be refused because of minor omissions, such as your address, so insist upon the provision of proper invoices by your suppliers.

Source: Regulation 14 of the VAT Regulations

VAT return checklist

Not only does VAT law change, but so will the transactions that go through your books and records. Thus what actually goes on a VAT return and what is left off can cause confusion. How can you consistently reduce the risk of making a mistake and incurring a penalty?

WHAT TO PUT ON YOUR VAT RETURN

The principle of VAT is that a business adds its output tax to its sales. If it sells to another VAT registered business, that business may claim relief for tax it has paid on its purchases and expenses (its input tax) against its own output tax. There are also different rates for different items, and a distinction between zero-rated items and exempt items.

INPUT TAX

The basic principle of claiming input tax is that you may claim for items that can be attributed, either directly or indirectly, to the taxable supplies you make. Generally, you can claim back input tax on business items. This may seem an obvious point but you would be surprised at the number of people who try to claim back VAT on private items. Plus, certain items are specifically excluded for the purposes of claiming input tax, such as VAT on cars, entertaining, and directors' accommodation.

OUTPUT TAX

For output tax, difficulties sometimes arise in deciding what is the correct rate of tax, and what constitutes a taxable supply. Then there is a problem with cars again. If you claim input tax relief on fuel for cars, and you have any private use during the VAT period, then you must add a scale charge to your output VAT on your VAT return.

So what actually goes on a VAT return and what is left off can cause confusion. Our **VAT Return Checklist** is a box-by-box guide to help you deal with any such decisions each time you complete a return.

VAT RETURN CHECKLIST

What goes on your VAT return?

Not only does VAT law change, but so do the transactions that go through your books and on to your records. So what's included on the VAT return, and what's left off, can cause confusion. This is a box-by-box guide to help you avoid the confusion.

Box 1 - OUTPUT VAT

As well as VAT on sales and other taxable business income you should include the VAT on:
- supplies to staff (vending machines, reduced price goods, etc.)
- sales of business assets and capital equipment
- motoring scale charges if you provide fuel for private use
- gifts of goods costing more than £50, excluding VAT
- the **full** value of goods sold in part-exchange
- commission received from selling other people's goods
- supplies of goods to unregistered customers in other EU member states
- self-billing invoices received
- any reverse charge services you receive (e.g. a German lawyer charges you £1,000 for work done in Germany; you charge yourself £150 (£1,000 x 15%) (will revert to 17.5% January 2010)
- errors in output VAT from earlier periods if the net amount is less than £10,000 (from July 1 2008) and deduct the VAT on any credit notes issued.

Box 2 - EU VAT

The VAT due on any acquisitions of goods from other member states of the EU (e.g. you buy some machinery from a supplier in Germany. He zero-rates the supply to you. The Sterling value of the goods is £1,000. You charge yourself £150 VAT (£1,000 x 15%) and put it in Box 2 as your output VAT (you claim it back in Box 4 though)).

Box 3 - SUB TOTAL

Add together the totals in boxes 1 and 2.

Box 4 - INPUT VAT

You should include:
- VAT reclaimable on purchases
- VAT on imports (taken from Customs Form C79 they send to you)
- acquisition tax accounted for in Box 2 (i.e. to cancel out the EU VAT)
- VAT on reverse charge services accounted for in Box 1
- VAT bad debt relief claims
- adjustments for credit notes received
- errors from earlier periods where the net amount is less than £10,000 (from July 1 2008).

You must exclude VAT on:
- the purchase of motor cars
- business entertainment
- goods bought under one of the second-hand schemes
- purchases for personal or private use
- purchases for non-business activities
- private accommodation for directors (but not hotel accommodation when away on business).

Box 5 - NET VAT

The net amount payable/receivable (Box 3 minus Box 4).

Box 6 - NET SALES

Include the total net value of outputs including:
- standard-rated supplies (including motoring scale charges)
- zero-rated supplies
- supplies to VAT registered businesses in other EU member states
- supplies to non-VAT registered customers in other EU member states
- supplies where the place of supply is outside the UK (e.g. a UK company buys goods from Hong Kong and has them delivered directly to a customer in Australia)
- own goods transferred to another EU member state
- sales to other EU member states on a sale or return basis
- deposits for which an invoice has been issued
- exports
- exempt supplies (e.g. insurance, financial services etc.)
- reverse charge transactions.

Box 7 - NET PURCHASES

The net value of purchases including:
- imports
- EU acquisitions
- reverse charge services.

You can exclude the following from Boxes 6 and 7:
- VAT itself
- wages, PAYE or NI
- money put into or taken out of the business by you
- loans, dividends and gifts of money
- insurance claims
- stock exchange dealings
- MOT certificates
- motor vehicle licence duty
- local authority rates
- income which is outside the scope of VAT because it is not consideration for a supply (e.g. compensation).

Box 8 - EU GOODS

The total value of goods (not services) supplied to other EU member states including:
- own goods transferred to another EU member state
- supplies to VAT registered businesses in other EU member states
- supplies to non-VAT registered customers in other EU member states
- goods transferred on consignment and "call-off" stock
- sales to other EU member states on a sale or return basis
- goods dispatched from the UK for installation or assembly in another EU member state
- supplies of new means of transport
- distance sales to unregistered customers (mail order) when you are above the registration threshold in the country of destination
- costs. The values should be in Sterling and include any related costs such as commission, packing transport, insurance etc.

Note. Everything in Box 8 should also be included in Box 6.

Box 9 - EU PURCHASES

The total value of acquisitions of goods from other EU member states, including:
- any goods brought to the UK from another EU member state even if no actual purchase takes place (e.g. goods transferred between divisions of the same company)
- goods assembled or installed in the UK that have been dispatched from another EU member state.

Note. Everything in Box 9 should also appear in Box 7 of the VAT return.

If you enclose a cheque with the return, remember to tick the box on the front of the form.

Voluntary disclosure letter

If you discover an error (before the VATman does) what should you do about it? Just let sleeping dogs lie, or confess all? If you do need to communicate with the VATman, how much detail do you realistically have to give him?

IF YOU FIND AN ERROR

If you discover that you've made a mistake and misdeclared the amount of VAT due, you need to adjust it. If the net error is less than £10,000 in total, you can adjust it on your next VAT return. However, remember to keep a record of the adjustment and how it was calculated, so you can show the VATman next time he pays you a visit. You should record: **(1)** the date the error was discovered; **(2)** the period in which it occurred; **(3)** whether it relates to input or output tax; and **(4)** where the supporting documents can be found. It's a good idea to annotate the adjustment on your VAT analysis with the words "voluntary disclosure adjustment".

If the error is more than £10,000, you have to tell the VATman in writing. You can do this by completing a VAT Form 652 and sending it to your local VAT office. Alternatively you could send a **Voluntary Disclosure Letter** with the details. The VATman will accept a voluntary disclosure any time before he begins "to make enquires", i.e. before he makes an appointment to inspect your records and in certain other limited circumstances.

VOLUNTARY DISCLOSURE LETTER

HMRC

Voluntary Disclosure Section

. . . . *(insert address)*

. . . .

. . . .

. . . .

. . . . *(insert date)*

. . . . *(insert your reference)*

Dear Sirs

. . . . ***(insert your business name)***

VRN. . . . . ***(insert your VAT registration number)***

Voluntary disclosure

We wish to advise the Commissioners of an error in accounting for . . . . . . *(insert details of the error)*. We have recently been advised that . . . . . *(insert details of the correct treatment)* and that VAT should have been accounted for on this transaction.

Accordingly we have enclosed a schedule of . . . . . . *(insert details of the error being declared)* together with the VAT due on these amounts.

If you have any queries please do not hesitate to contact us.

Yours faithfully

. . . . *(insert name)*

Enc

..............................*(insert your business name)*

VRN..........................*(insert your VAT registration number)*

Voluntary Disclosure: schedule of errors

......*(insert output/input)* tax not accounted for on .....*(insert the transaction).*

VAT return period	Net amount (£)	VAT (£)
Total ([under]/[over] declared)		

Written rulings letter

If you have a problem you could ring the VATman for an answer and follow his advice. Then, when he comes to visit you a couple of years later and asks why you are doing things this way you can tell him. But the ever sympathetic VATman may ask, if you have a note of the conversation, or a letter confirming the ruling.

OBTAINING A WRITTEN RULING

If you have no evidence supporting an unusual VAT treatment you have adopted, then the VATman will assess back for up to three years to correct this "error".

The VATman now runs a National Advice Service, which provides a telephone helpline that can be contacted on 0845 010 9000. The standard of advice is at best variable, but is OK for basic queries. If you need advice on anything else, ask for it in writing using the **Written Rulings Letter**. There are a number of advice centres around the country dealing with written enquiries, and you can obtain the address of your nearest one from the above mentioned National Advice Service. Again, the standard of advice is not great, and you will normally only get the VATman's view of the law. But if you provide him with all the facts and get a written ruling, he will have to stick by it, even if the advice is wrong. All he will be able to do is make you do it correctly in future - so no assessment!

EXCUSES, EXCUSES

It's not always that easy to get a written ruling from the VATman. His published guidance states: "You can write to us and ask for our view on how a particular transaction that has taken place, or is due to occur shortly, should be treated for VAT". However, he has a get-out clause that says he will not answer hypothetical questions. He has been known to use this excuse to dodge answering difficult questions, but if you persevere he will give you a ruling. If the VATman is initially unwilling to give a written answer, threaten him with the Adjudicator. This usually concentrates his mind. Don't worry, we've included suitable wording in our letter to cover just such an eventuality.

WRITTEN RULINGS LETTER

(Written rulings centre obtained from National Advice Service)

. . . . *(insert address)*

. . . .

. . . .

. . . .

. . . . *(insert date)*

. . . . *(insert your reference)*

Dear Sirs

. . . . ***(insert your business name)***

VRN. . . . . ***(insert your VAT registration number)***

Request for Written Ruling

We are writing to ask for your view on how a particular transaction that *(has taken place or is due to occur shortly)* should be treated for VAT in accordance with the VAT Enquiries Guide - VAT Leaflet 700/51. Please note this is not a hypothetical question.

. . . .

. . . .

. . . .

. . . .

(provide the VATman with all the facts of the transaction).

If you are unable to provide me with a written ruling then we will consider referring the matter to the Adjudicator.

If you have any queries please do not hesitate to contact us.

Yours faithfully

. . . . *(insert name)*

Option to tax letter

Renting is normally exempt from VAT. This means that no VAT is payable, but you can't normally recover any of the VAT incurred on your expenses. However, you can "opt to tax", charging VAT on rent/sale of the property and recover any VAT you have or will incur. So what do you need to do?

RECLAIMING VAT ON PROPERTY

When you register for VAT, i.e. opt to tax, as long as you have an appropriate invoice, you can recover this input VAT on your first VAT return. But what about services incurred more than six months ago, which have an ongoing benefit, such as building works?

If you own a property (or grant a lease), you can opt to charge VAT on it, otherwise it will be treated as exempt from VAT. You would probably make such an election using our **Option to Tax Letter** if you had incurred major expenditure on the property, such as during a refurbishment. In this situation, if you don't charge VAT, you can't reclaim the VAT you have incurred on the expenditure. Of course, if the VAT costs are small you might not bother. This is a particularly complex piece of legislation, so seek expert VAT advice early on in any property deal.

When a business decides that it wants to opt to tax a building (charge VAT on the rent or sale) it is then able to recover the VAT on any related costs.

However, if you have already charged rent (exempt from VAT) on the property and now want to charge VAT and recover old input VAT, e.g. on the original purchase of the building or a recent renovation or reconstruction, then you have to obtain permission from the VATman to do so and propose a suitable method of partial recovery as part of the process.

EXAMPLE

Let's say you bought a commercial building for £200,000 plus VAT (£30,000) two years ago and rented it out for this period before opting to tax. You are blocked from recovering VAT that relates to the exempt period, i.e. two years' worth of that £30,000. The question is how do you calculate this amount?

When apportioning make sure you get the best deal possible and don't let the VATman get away with anything. Where he ignores the legislation and makes up his own rules then, depending on the amount of VAT involved, appeal to the VAT Tribunal. It usually follows the legislation and ignores rules made up by the VATman with no legal basis.

OPTION TO TAX LETTER

HMRC

. . . .*(insert address)*

. . . .

. . . .

. . . .

. . . .*(insert date)*

. . . .*(insert your reference)*

Dear Sirs

. . . .***(insert your business name)***

VRN . . . .***(insert your VAT registration number)***

Please accept this letter as written notification of our intention to waive the exemption in respect of the property and land situated at . . . . . *(insert full address details of the land and property)* under the terms of **Para 2, Schedule 10, VAT Act 1994**.

The election is to take effect from . . . . . *(insert date)* and we would be grateful if you would acknowledge receipt of the election.

We confirm that no exempt supplies have been made in respect of these land and buildings.

Yours faithfully

. . . .*(insert name)*

Repayment letter

The VATman's very quick to charge you interest (or even a penalty) if you don't pay him on time. However, if you are in the lucky situation of being due a repayment of VAT can you legitimately kick up a fuss, if he delays in handing back your cash?

VAT REPAYMENTS

Provided you send in your VAT return on time, the VATman must repay any VAT due to you no later than 30 days after he receives it. The sooner you send in the return, the sooner he will have to repay you, direct to your bank account. But the VATman does have one get-out clause. If he wants to look into the reasons for an unusual repayment, he can stop the 30-day clock whilst he makes reasonable enquiries about the repayment that's due. What does this mean? Reasonable enquiries means a visit to make sure that you're entitled to the refund.

Although the VATman doesn't do this with every repayment, he's suspicious by nature and it's quite common for unusual repayments to be queried. However, if the information required to resolve the query is held by the VATman, either centrally (where the VAT returns go) or locally, the 30-day clock does not stop. So it's best to write to the VATman using our **Repayment Letter** giving details about what has led to the repayment claim. Include copies of purchase invoices and the relevant purchase day book/print out if necessary. Send a copy of the letter with your VAT return (in case it gets lost centrally) and send another copy to your local VAT office. By doing this the VATman has all the information to resolve the repayment query and he'll have no excuse to delay your repayment or more importantly, to make a visit.

REPAYMENT LETTER

HMRC

. . . .*(insert address)*

. . . .

. . . .

. . . .

. . . .*(insert date)*

. . . .*(insert your reference)*

Dear Sirs

. . . .***(insert your business name)***

VRN . . . .***(insert your VAT registration number)***

Reasons For Repayment

We wish to advise the Commissioners of the reasons why a repayment has appeared on the VAT return for the VAT return period . . . . *(insert period)*. This was due to . . . . *(insert reasons for significant input VAT claim)*.

Accordingly we have enclosed a schedule of . . . . *(insert the transactions)* together with the VAT on these amounts. Also enclosed is a photocopy of the relevant invoice(s).

If you have any queries please do not hesitate to contact us.

Yours faithfully

. . . .*(insert name)*

Enc

Appeal letter

If you think that you have a good case against the VATman, you can take him to tribunal to resolve a dispute. Sometimes even the threat of tribunal will get him to see sense and negotiate.

Resolving disagreements

In our experience, small businesses often receive inaccurate assessments for relatively small sums (under £10,000).

If you disagree with the VATman over an assessment, you can ask for an Internal Review of the decision or you can appeal to a VAT tribunal. The VATman advises that in the first instance you should write to your local office and formally ask for an Internal Review. This is where an experienced, usually senior, officer reviews an assessment or decision. If clearly inaccurate, it will usually be withdrawn, or reduced. This review must be completed within 45 days or a longer period if you agree to it.

But you still don't have to take the VATman's advice. Instead, make sure that you enter an appeal to the Tribunal Service (Tax) using their official Notice of Appeal. An appeal needs to be entered within 30 days of the disputed decision by the VATman, which is normally the date of the assessment (but not the date it was received). Once you have entered a formal appeal use our **Appeal Letter**. Your professional costs will be paid if the tribunal decides that the VATman acted unreasonably in the conduct of your case.

APPEAL LETTER

Tribunal Service (Tax)
2nd Floor
54 Hagley Road
Birmingham
B16 8PE

. . . . *(insert date)*

. . . . *(insert your reference)*

Dear Sirs

. . . . ***(insert your business name)***

VRN . . . . ***(insert your VAT registration number)***

Please find enclosed a duly completed Notice of Appeal relating to assessment made by the Commissioners on . . . . *(insert date of assessment)*.

We have enclosed a copy of the assessment for your information.

If you have any queries please do not hesitate to contact us.

Yours faithfully

. . . . *(insert name)*

. . . . *(insert company name)*

Enc

Internal Review letter

In resolving disputed assessments Internal Review is the name given to the process whereby a different VAT officer reviews an assessment (or decision). However, you have to ask for this to happen.

GETTING AN ASSESSMENT CHANGED

If you disagree with the VATman over an assessment, you can ask for an Internal Review of the decision or you can appeal to a VAT tribunal. The VATman advises that in the first instance you should write to your local office and formally ask for and Internal Review. This is where an experienced, usually senior, officer reviews an assessment or decision. If clearly inaccurate, it will usually be withdrawn, or reduced. The review must be completed within 45 days or a longer period if you agree to it.

However, if after the threat of a tribunal the VATman withdraws the assessment, you can withdraw your tribunal appeal.

INTERNAL REVIEW

HMRC

Internal Review Officer

. . . . *(insert address)*

. . . .

. . . .

. . . . *(insert date)*

. . . . *(insert your reference)*

Dear Sirs

. . . . ***(insert your business name)***

VRN . . . .***(insert your VAT registration number)***

. . . . ***(insert assessment number)***

We are writing to request a formal Internal Review of an assessment for £. . . . . *(insert amount of assessment)* plus interest issued by the Commissioners on . . . . . *(insert date of assessment)*.

Background

(. . . . .)

Grounds for review

(. . . . .)

The supporting evidence is available.

Accordingly we would request that the Commissioners withdraw their assessment.

If you have any queries please do not hesitate to contact us.

Yours faithfully

. . . . *(insert name)*

. . . . *(insert company name)*

Compensation claim letter

Chances are, that sometime in your dealings with the VATman, he will give you an incorrect ruling, issue an inaccurate assessment or his internal admin systems won't work properly. Can you claim compensation for the cost of this inconvenience?

MAKING A COMPLAINT

Let's say the VATman comes to call and later issues you with an assessment. You feel that he is wrong and obtain professional advice. The advisor agrees that the assessment is incorrect. The advisor puts in an appeal to the tribunal asking for an Internal Review of the assessment. The VATman sees the error of his ways and withdraws the assessment in full. The advisor claims his costs from the VATman and everything seems to be resolved. A win, win for you!

However, the VATman's computer starts sending you reminders to pay the (withdrawn) assessment. The VATman has got his wires crossed and the various sections involved are not communicating with each other. This is not a matter that can be appealed to a tax tribunal, so what can you do? First, find out the address of the Regional Complaints Unit (from the Customs helpline on 0845 010 9000) and write to them making a formal complaint of the way the matter has been handled.

PROFESSIONAL COSTS

If you have incurred professional costs in obtaining advice on how to handle a matter, or have got your accountant/tax advisor to deal with it for you, you can ask the VATman for an ex gratia payment to cover the costs. The local office can authorise payments of up to £900 without referring the matter to higher authority. They are usually quite good at making these local payments, mainly because it closes the matter before it is referred to the independent Adjudicator. However, if you do not take a hard line in these matters they can run on for months and cause considerable aggravation.

Use the **Compensation Claim Letter** to claim your professional costs back by writing to the Solicitors' Office with a detailed breakdown of the time costs, including time taken to prepare the claim. It will take the VATman two to three months to agree the claim for costs and send you a cheque. However, he will not pay your personal time costs so don't handle the Notice of Appeal yourself, get professional help right from the beginning.

COMPENSATION CLAIM LETTER

HMRC

. . . . *(insert address)*

. . . .

. . . .

. . . . *(insert date)*

. . . . *(insert your reference)*

Dear Sirs

. . . . ***(insert your business name)***

VRN . . . . ***(insert your VAT registration number)***

We attach a detailed costs claim.

The Commissioners issued an assessment for £. . . . *(insert amount of assessment)* plus interest on . . . . . *(insert date)*.

. . . . . *(insert your company name)* appealed against this assessment on . . . . . *(insert date of your appeal letter)* which was subsequently withdrawn following negotiations with the Commissioners.

The attached costs claim has been compiled from documents retained on our files covering the period from the date the appeal was lodged to the date it was withdrawn.

We would be grateful if you would review the attached and confirm that the Commissioners are prepared to reimburse our client for the costs incurred in negotiating the withdrawal of the assessment.

If you have any queries regarding this matter, please contact us.

Yours faithfully

. . . . *(insert name)*

. . . . *(insert company name)*

Enc

.... *(insert your business name)*

VRN .... *(insert your VAT registration number)*

Details of costs claim

Charge rates:

Description	Rate	Reference
(Advisor 1)	£ X per hour	A1
(Advisor 2)	£ X per hour	A2

Calculation of costs:

Date	Description	Amount
	Telephone conversation; e-mail regarding receipt of assessment disallowing .... *(insert subject of assessment)*.	A1 - 0.75 hours = £... **Total £...**
	Discussions regarding recent Tribunal decisions regarding similar cases.	A1 - 0.25 hours = £... A2 - 0.25 hours = £... **Total £...**
	Telephone call to client. Discussions regarding background. E-mail receipt of faxed information relevant papers.	A1 - 0.5 hours = £... **Total £...**
	Research and preparation time, starting to draft reconsideration letter. E-mailing draft to client.	A1 - 2.75 hours = £... **Total £...**
	Further conversations with client, receipt of additional information by fax and e-mail regarding under-declared output VAT, preparing an Internal Review letter and schedule. Completion of the Tribunal Service's Notice of Appeal and covering letter.	A1 - 1.75 hours = £.... **Total £...**
	Receipt of Commissioners' letter withdrawing assessment. Letter to the Tribunal withdrawing Appeal.	A1 - 0.75 hours = £... **Total £...**
	Draft costs claim and covering letter.	A1 - 1.5 hours = £... **Total £...**
Total claim for costs		**£ X, XXX.XX**

Reasonable excuse letter

The VATman has a wide range of penalties available to him. Many of these can be mitigated (reduced) while others can be removed completely if you have a reasonable excuse. What might your reasonable excuse be?

HAVING A REASONABLE EXCUSE

Most of the penalties imposed by the VATman will be cancelled in full if the taxpayer can establish a "reasonable excuse" defence. Unhelpfully though, there is no definition of "reasonable excuse". This argument now applies to: **(1)** failure to notify liability; and **(2)** default surcharge.

In relation to failure to notify liability to registration, the situations where a reasonable excuse can be established are: **(1)** compassionate circumstances; **(2)** transferring a business as a going concern; **(3)** doubt as to the liability of supplies; or **(4)** uncertainty of employment status. With the default surcharge, there is a different list including: **(1)** computer breakdown; **(2)** illness of key personnel; **(3)** unexpected cash crisis; or **(4)** loss of records.

Excuses that won't work are: **(1)** holidays - cheque signatories being on holiday and not being able to write out the VAT cheque; **(2)** pregnancy - "our bookkeeper went into hospital to have her baby that week" - it has been tried and failed; and **(3)** no loss - the fact that there has been no significant loss of VAT.

IGNORANCE OF THE LAW

Ignorance of the law is not mentioned in the VATman's lists although it is relevant to both failure to notify and the misdeclaration penalty. For example, in the case of **Nicols** a distinction was made between basic ignorance in relation to registering for VAT and his ignorance of the fact that expenses incurred abroad and charged to his customers would be regarded as part of his turnover for VAT. The issue has been raised in relation to:
- liability of particular supplies
- whether supplies are made in the course of business
- place of supply
- time of supply
- supplies involving agents or subcontractors

- the existence of a partnership
- imports
- bad debts; and
- credit notes.

USE A LETTER

The conclusion is that you can put forward different reasons for different penalties. To convey an excuse to the VATman use our **Reasonable Excuse Letter**.

If all else fails, haggle. Don't give up without a fight. If your argument does not constitute a reasonable excuse it may go some way towards it and warrant a reduction in the penalty. Practice has shown that haggling does work.

REASONABLE EXCUSE LETTER

HMRC

Internal Review Officer

. . . . *(insert address)*

. . . .

. . . .

. . . . *(insert date)*

. . . . *(insert your reference)*

Dear Sirs

. . . . ***(insert your business name)***

VRN . . . . ***(insert your VAT registration number)***

Reasonable Excuse for Late Submission of a VAT Return

We are writing to request a formal reconsideration of the penalty £ . . . . *(insert figure)* within the assessment . . . . . *(insert assessment reference)* for £ . . . . *(insert amount of assessment)* plus interest issued by the Commissioners on . . . . . *(insert date of assessment)*.

The grounds for this request are that we had a "reasonable excuse" for the VAT return (and/or payment) for the period . . . . . *(insert period of late return)* being submitted late. The reasonable excuse is . . . . . *(insert details)*.

Supporting evidence is available.

Accordingly we would request that the Commissioners withdraw or reduce the penalty imposed.

If you have any queries please do not hesitate to contact us.

Yours faithfully

. . . . *(insert name)*

Authority letter to the VATman

Exchanges between advisors and the VATman have, in the past, failed to reduce matters because the VATman says he can't reveal confidential information about your business (although he might lose it!). What can you do to make sure things run smoothly?

GETTING AROUND A CONFIDENTIALITY ISSUE

The Taxman isn't allowed to reveal confidential information to a tax advisor/accountant unless he holds the authority to do so. However, although the Taxman and VATman have merged into Her Majesty's Revenue and Customs (HMRC), any existing authority held by the Taxman doesn't work for VAT correspondence. For example, appeals to the VATman against a late filing penalty have been rejected because he did not hold a direct authority from the taxpayer.

HMRC has finally produced a combined authority document (New Form 64-8). This allows you to state which taxes the advisor will be dealing with, including VAT. However (pending the processing of an new 64-8 you may have submitted), we suggest sending in an **Authority Letter to the VATman** along with the next appeal/correspondence. This is to avoid the hassle of the appeal being rejected or the VATman refusing to answer your advisor's letters.

AUTHORITY LETTER TO THE VATMAN

. . . . *(insert address)*

. . . .

. . . .

. . . . *(insert date)*

Dear Sir

I, ... *(insert name and VAT number of the trader)* authorise HMRC to disclose VAT information held about my business affairs to . . . . *(insert name and address of nominee)* who is acting on my behalf.

This authorisation covers all VAT matters within the responsibility of HMRC and includes approaches which may be made to obtain information from all sections of the department, such as the National Advice Service, Debt Management Unit, National Registration Service and Complaints Unit. This authority will remain in force until I give you written notice to the contrary.

Yours faithfully

. . . . *(signature)*

. . . . *(insert your name)*

. . . . *(insert date)*

Chapter 7

Capital Gains Tax

Calculation of CGT pro forma

Do you know how much of a gain you've made for Capital Gains Tax (CGT) purposes on, say, your shares? Do you have any asset on which you could establish a capital loss in order to offset these gains? To answer these and other CGT planning questions we suggest that you start with a CGT pro forma calculation amongst your tax papers.

LEGAL DEDUCTIONS

When you sell your assets you might have to pay CGT on any profit you make. But there are loads of legal deductions that can reduce the taxable gain.

The gain is usually calculated by taking the actual disposal proceeds and deducting the purchase cost. Remember to deduct all the costs of sale and purchase, including broker's/agent's fees. Keep all this information with your tax papers.

Use our **Calculation of CGT Pro Forma** to estimate your capital gain.

CALCULATION OF CGT PRO FORMA

Description of asset:

Business asset? No

	Date (MM/YY)	£	£
Disposal proceeds			
Less:	Purchase cost		
	Enhancement expenditure		
Gain			
Less:	Annual exemption (if not used elsewhere)		(10,100)
Taxable gain			
Tax @ 18%			

Share valuation pro forma

Do you know how much the shares in your company are worth? Apart from being in the "it's nice to know" category, this might become essential knowledge in your dealings with the Taxman over share transfers. But how can you easily prove the most beneficial value for tax purposes?

GIFTING ASSETS

If you make a gift of an asset, shares for example, to anyone other than your spouse, it's deemed to have been made at fair market value and will be liable to CGT as if an actual gain has been made. This can be unattractive as you haven't actually made a gain, and won't have received any money.

However, if you are giving away a business asset, you can claim gift (or holdover) relief. This relief defers the CGT on the gift by transferring the liability to the recipient. When the recipient eventually sells the gift, the full CGT bill will normally fall due, but the recipient, rather than you, will have to pay for it. You can use the Taxman's form IR295 to make the claim for gift relief, but you need to declare the market value when gifted.

So, each time you gift/transfer shares in your trading company you will need to value these shares. Use our **Share Valuation Pro Forma** as a valuable guide to establishing the right figure for you, but also seek advice from your accountant.

SHARE VALUATION PRO FORMA

Company name: . . . .

Valuation date: . . . .

Percentage shareholding: . . . .

Step 1 - Calculating "Super" profits

	Year ended March 31			
	2009	**2008**	**2007**	**2006**
	£	**£**	**£**	**£**
Profit per accounts (prior to dividends but after tax)	100,000	90,000	80,000	70,000
Add back:				
Directors' remuneration	30,000	30,000	30,000	30,000
Directors' NI	3,234	3,248	2,994	3,032
Other items that have distorted profit:	-	-	-	-
e.g. One-off loss				
Adjusted profit	133,234	123,248	112,994	103,032
Less:				
Manager's salary (include a manager's salary for each working director)	40,000	40,000	40,000	40,000
Employers' NI on Manager's salary	4,514	4,528	4,174	4,222
Other items that have distorted profit:	-	-	-	-
e.g. Capital Gain				
"Super" Profits (unweighted)	88,720	78,720	68,820	58,810
Weighting (more weight given to most recent results)	4	3	2	
Weighted Average Super Profits	78,749			

Step 2 - Calculating the value of the company

Weighted Average Super profit (A)	Estimated P/E ratio (B)	Value of company (AxB)
£	(Range usually 2.5 to 5)	£
78,749	3	236,247

Step 3 - Valuation of actual shareholding

	£	£
5% shareholding	236,247	11,812
Less:		
Discount for minority shareholding:	50%	5,906
Valuation		**11,812**

Rollover relief claim

Whether you've sold an asset under the old CGT taper relief rules or the new 18% flat rate rules, and this still leaves you with a substantial gain, there is something you can do. If you are willing to re-invest the proceeds in a new business or business asset, then a rollover relief claim may be used to defer the gain.

SELLING A BUSINESS

CGT is due on any profit you make when you sell a business. However, you can control when you pay this tax.

Disposals pre-April 6 2008

If you've owned the business for more than two years, then the gain will automatically be reduced by 75% due to taper relief. However, if this still leaves you with a substantial gain and you are willing to re-invest the proceeds in a new business or business asset, then a **Rollover Relief Claim** can be used to defer the gain.

Rollover relief isn't just available on the sale and purchase of business goodwill, it can also be claimed for land and buildings and fixed plant and machinery as long as they were/are actually used in your business. Unfortunately, it isn't possible to claim this relief on the sale of shares in a family company, but that doesn't stop you selling the assets in the company and claiming the relief.

The gain is said to be rolled over because it is deducted from the cost of the replacement asset, therefore increasing its potential gain. The replacement asset must be acquired within a period starting one year before and three years after the date of the disposal of the original asset. If you only re-invest part of the proceeds, then the relief will be restricted to the amount re-invested.

Disposals post-April 6 2008

Entrepreneurs' relief can apply when you sell part or all of your business, or shares in your own company after April 5 2008. The capital gain will be reduced to five-ninths of the full gain, making the effective CGT rate 10%. So the taper relief position (75% discount on the gain) is restored if all the new relief conditions are met.

For example, you sell the shares in your company for a gain of £450,000. Entrepreneurs' relief reduces the gain to £250,000 (5/9 x £450,000). The tax due is £45,000 (18% x £250,000), an effective rate of 10% on the full gain of £450,000. You can also deduct your annual exemption, (£10,100 for 2009/10) and any capital losses from the taxable gain to reduce your tax bill even further.

You must have held the shares or assets for at least a year before the sale, and the business must be trading, so property letting businesses don't qualify. Where you sell a company, you must own at least 5% of the voting ordinary shares, and have either worked in, or been an officer of, the company or an associated company.

£1 MILLION CAP

There is no minimum age limit on the entrepreneurs' relief, so you don't have to "retire" when you sell your business to qualify. But there is a lifetime limit of £1 million of gains that can be subject to the relief. This means you can make a number of gains totalling £1 million over several years, and claim entrepreneurs' relief on them all, but any gains in excess of £1 million will be taxed at the full 18%.

There will be rules to prevent income, normally taxed at rates of up to 40%, being presented as gains to be taxed at 18%, but at the time of publication these had not yet been made available.

However, if this still leaves you with a substantial gain and you are willing to re-invest the proceeds in a new business or business asset, then a **Rollover Relief Claim** may be used to defer the gain.

ROLLOVER RELIEF CLAIM

HMRC

. . . . *(insert address)*

. . . .

. . . .

. . . .

. . . . *(insert date)*

Dear Sirs

. . . . ***(insert your name)***

. . . . ***(insert your ten digit tax reference)***

. . . . *(insert business name or asset description)* was sold for £ . . . . . *(insert sale proceeds)* on . . . . . . *(insert date)*. Proceeds of £ . . . . *(insert amount re-invested)* were reinvested in the purchase of . . . . *(insert new business name or asset description)* on . . . . . *(insert date)*. Both the asset sold and the asset acquired fall into the class of assets set out in s.155 of the **Taxation of Chargeable Gains Act 1992**.

Please accept this letter as a formal claim under s.152 of the Taxation of Chargeable Gains Act 1992 that the chargeable gain arising on the disposal is rolled over and that the base cost is reduced accordingly.

Yours faithfully

. . . . *(insert signature)*

Extra statutory concession (ESC) 16 form

For whatever reason, you've decided to wind the company up. Strangely enough there's a way the Taxman can help you save costs on this process. However, you have to ask him nicely and provide all the right documentation.

WINDING UP A COMPANY

If you've sold the assets rather than the shares in your company, and you now want to shut it down, you have two options. You can either go into expensive voluntary liquidation or you can opt for a more informal and cheaper form of winding up by completing form 652a available from Companies House. However, before you can do this you need to get the Taxman's permission and give him certain assurances by using the **Extra Statutory Concession (ESC) 16 Form**. If you are granted ESC16, then any payments made to you and any other shareholders during the winding up will be treated as capital rather than dividend income.

EXTRA STATUTORY CONCESSION (ESC)16 FORM

. . . . *(insert company name)* LIMITED

ESC16 Dissolution of Company under s.652, **Companies Act 1985**:

Distribution of Shareholders of . . . . . *(insert company name)* Limited.

The Company makes an application under extra statutory concession 16 to make a distribution of assets to its shareholders.

The Company:

1. Has ceased to trade.

2. Intends to collect its debts, pay off its creditors and distribute any balance of assets to its shareholders.

3. Intends to seek striking off.

4. Intends to make a prudent interim capital distribution before finalising the affairs of the company.

The company and its shareholders agree that:

1. They will supply such information as is necessary to determine, and will pay, any Corporation Tax liability on income and capital gains, any Advance Corporation Tax liability on distributions under **Schedule 13 ICTA 1998**: and

2. The shareholders will pay any Capital Gains Tax liability in respect of any amount distributed to them in cash or otherwise as if the distributions had been made during a winding up.

On behalf of company and shareholders.

. . . . *(insert signature)*

. . . . *(insert date)*

Calculation of goodwill pro forma

When you transfer a business to a limited company, you need to calculate the value of the goodwill in it. If the Taxman doesn't agree with your valuation, the difference between his (lower) and your (higher) valuation will be taxed on you. What documents do you need in place to avoid this potential tax problem?

INCORPORATING A BUSINESS

You may have started as a sole trader or a partnership, but have now decided to incorporate your business. When you transfer a business to a limited company, you need to calculate the value of the goodwill in it. The larger the goodwill figure, the more money you take out of the company tax-free. As you are gifting business assets, you can claim gift relief on the transfer and therefore defer any CGT liability on the gain.

Use our **Calculation of Goodwill Pro Forma** to estimate the value of goodwill in your business. You should also include a price adjuster clause in your valuation so that the figure can be automatically varied if the Taxman doesn't agree, avoiding the possible problem of any difference between his (lower) and your (higher) valuation being treated as taxable income. It's best to ask the Taxman to agree your valuation by completing form CG34 (http://www.hmrc.gov.uk/forms/cg34. pdf).

CALCULATION OF GOODWILL PRO FORMA

Name . . . .

T/A . . . .

Calculation of goodwill as at . . . . *(insert date)*

                                                 £   £

Profit history (sole trader or partnership)

Year-ended . . . .

Year-ended . . . .

Year-ended . . . .

Average annual profit (last three years)

Profit projection (Company)

Estimated projected maintainable profits

Yield on capital investment

Net assets (excluding cash)

Yield (say base rate + 1.25%)

Calculation of super profits

Estimated projected maintainable profits

Less: Yield on capital investment

Less: Deemed manager's salary

Super profit

Goodwill calculation

Assume 2.5 multiplier

Less: Personal element (say 20%)

Goodwill valuation agreed

Note:

We believe the following factors create a conservative valuation:

1. Maintainable profits.

2. Manager's salary.

3. Multiplier.

4. Personal goodwill.

Price adjuster clause

Should the parties become aware that a fair market price is different from this figure, the price shall be adjusted accordingly.

Claim for loss on irrecoverable

loan to a trader

Obviously, if you sell a capital asset for less than you bought it, this will create a capital loss, all of which will be confirmed by the sale documentation. However, if you've made a loan to a business which can't repay it, you might be able to claim a capital loss on this too. So what documentation will you need to be successful with this particular claim?

CAPITAL LOSSES - IRRECOVERABLE LOAN

One way to reduce your CGT bill is to offset capital losses against your capital gains. But there are other ways of creating a capital loss that you may not be aware of. For example, have you ever made a loan to a business? If you have, and the loan has subsequently been written off, then it may be treated as a capital loss. This doesn't happen automatically, so you will need to submit a **Claim for Loss on Irrecoverable Loan to a Trader**. The loan will qualify for loss relief as long as it was used by the borrower (who can't be your spouse) in their trade and the Taxman can satisfy himself that you haven't waived your right to recover the loan. Strictly speaking, the relief is due only when a claim is made, but in practice the Taxman permits claims to be made within two years of the year of assessment that you are claiming the loss relief for.

CLAIM FOR LOSS ON IRRECOVERABLE LOAN TO A TRADER

HMRC

. . . . *(insert address)*

. . . .

. . . .

. . . .

. . . . *(insert date)*

Dear Sirs

. . . . ***(insert your name)***

. . . . ***(insert your ten digit tax reference)***

I hereby claim capital loss relief under the provisions of s.253(3) of the **Taxation of Chargeable Gains Act 1992** in respect of a loan of £ . . . . *(insert loan amount)*, made to . . . . *(insert name and address of trader / trading company)* for use in his trade on the grounds that the loan has now become irrecoverable.

Yours faithfully

. . . . *(insert signature)*

Claim for payment under a guarantee

One way of helping a growing business is to act as guarantor to their loan finance. If things don't turn out as planned and you are called upon to make good some or all of the loan can you claim anything against your own personal tax bill?

CAPITAL LOSSES - PAYMENT UNDER A GUARANTEE

You might want to establish a capital loss to offset against any capital gains you have made in the tax year. Acting as a guarantor may be one way of doing this that you weren't aware of.

Business angels sometimes guarantee other people's loans as well as making them themselves. Indeed, you may have been one of these for a start-up business. For example, let's say you've given personal guarantees in respect of a bank loan to your friend's company. If the business can't repay the loan, then the bank will call on you to pay the amount due. In these circumstances, you may be able to submit a **Claim for Payment Under a Guarantee** and have the amount of the payment treated as a capital loss. This claim must be submitted within five years after the January 31 following the year of assessment.

CLAIM FOR PAYMENT UNDER A GUARANTEE

HMRC

. . . .*(insert address)*

. . . .

. . . .

. . . .

. . . .*(insert date)*

Dear Sirs

. . . .**(insert your name)**

. . . .**(insert your ten digit tax reference)**

I hereby claim capital loss relief under the provisions of s.253(4) of the **Taxation of Chargeable Gains Act 1992** in respect of a payment of £ . . . . . . *(insert payment amount)*, made under a guarantee in respect of a bank loan made to . . . . *(insert name and address of trader / trading company)* for use in his trade. The payment was a result of a formal calling in of the guarantee by . . . . *(insert bank name / address)*.

Yours faithfully

. . . .*(insert signature)*

Negligible value claim

Shares sometimes take a nosedive in value. It happens. However, if your investment's price goes through the floor do you have to sell it to claim the obvious loss for tax purposes? Or is there another way of proving to the Taxman that you've taken a hit, for CGT purposes.

LOSSES ON SHARES

You may have made an investment in the past that has performed badly. Indeed, you may have written it off in your own mind, but if you haven't sold it, it may only be a paper loss that is not allowable for CGT purposes. However, there is an exception to the normal rule whereby you may be able to establish an allowable capital loss to offset against a capital gain even though there hasn't been an actual disposal. If you can persuade the Taxman that the shares are virtually worthless, you can offset this loss against your capital gains to reduce the amount of CGT you pay.

The Taxman keeps a list of quoted shares that are recognised as being of negligible value (see http://hmrc.gov.uk/cgt/negligible_list.htm). You can make a **Negligible Value Claim** for the shares to be treated as though you sold them on the date you made the claim or up to two years before the tax year in which you make the claim (as long as they were worthless at the time). You can make a negligible value claim at any time after the shares have become worthless. Therefore, defer a claim until there are sufficient gains to avoid you wasting your annual exemption (£10,100 for 2009/10).

NEGLIGIBLE VALUE CLAIM

HMRC

.............................*(insert address)*

....

....

....

.............................*(insert date)*

Dear Sirs

Negligible value claim

.............................***(insert your name)***

.............................***(insert your ten digit tax reference)***

I claim relief under s.24(2) of the **Taxation of Chargeable Gains Act 1992** for the tax year ended April 5 . . . . . *(insert year)* in respect of my shareholding in . . . . . . *(insert company name)* plc which cost £. . . . . *(insert figure)*.

*[The shares are included on the "negligible value list" maintained by the Shares Valuation Office and were of negligible value as at the date of this claim].

*[The shares are not currently included on the "negligible value list" maintained by the Shares Valuation Office, but I believe the shares are of negligible value and would ask the Shares Valuation Office to consider including them on the list].

Please could you acknowledge receipt of this claim.

Yours faithfully

delete as appropriate

Trading loss relief claim

One of the best tax reliefs you can claim is to offset a loss from one of your income sources against your total taxable income, rather than having to wait and use it against future profits from that same source. You don't get this automatically; you have to put in a specific election to do so with the Taxman. Here's how you can do this with sole trader or partnership losses.

TRADING LOSSES

You can't offset capital losses against your general income in a tax year. However, you can reduce your capital gains by offsetting sole trader or partnership trading losses which you haven't been able to offset against other income.

This **Trading Loss Relief Claim** should not be made on its own - it should be made at the same time as a claim to offset the current year's trading loss against other total income for the year of loss and/or the previous tax year ("s.64 claim"). The claim must be made within twelve months of January 31 following the end of the tax year in which the loss arose.

A s.64 claim against income of the year must be made first, in full, up to the amount of other income (unfortunately, in many instances this can result in the personal allowance being wasted).

The amount of the trading loss then remaining to be utilised against the capital gain is the lower of the "relevant amount" and the "maximum amount". The "relevant amount" is the amount of trading loss that is left over after the s.64 claim has been dealt with (possibly because there is not enough income to fully utilise the loss); the "maximum amount" is the amount of capital gains arising in the year less the capital losses of the same year and unrelieved capital losses brought forward. Once that lower amount has been calculated, it is allowed in the computation before other capital losses brought forward or carried back and definitely before the annual exemption (which may, again, be wasted).

TRADING LOSS RELIEF CLAIM

HMRC

. . . . *(insert address)*

. . . .

. . . .

. . . .

. . . . *(insert date)*

Dear Sirs

. . . . ***(insert your name)***

. . . . ***(insert your ten digit tax reference)***

In the tax year ended April 5 . . . *(insert year)*, my business made a loss of £ . . . . . . *(insert amount)*. In accordance with the provisions of s.64(2) **ITA 2007**, I elect £ . . . . *(insert amount)* of this loss to be offset against my other income in the tax year ended April 5 . . . *(insert year)*.

In the tax year ended April 5 . . . . *(insert year)*, I also made capital gains (after deducting allowable losses but before deducting taper relief) of £. . . . . *(insert amount)*. In accordance with the provisions of s.71 **ITA 2007**, I elect for £ . . . . . *(insert amount)* of the trading loss to be offset against these gains.

Please could you acknowledge receipt of this claim.

Yours faithfully

. . . . *(insert signature)*

Chapter 8

Property investment

Rental income and expenditure account

To reduce the amount of rental profit, and consequently the amount of tax you pay, you need to claim as many expenses as possible. So how do you keep track of these expenses?

RENTAL INCOME

For income tax purposes, property investment is treated as a business and, therefore, net rental income is calculated in broadly the same way as self-employed business profits. To work out your net rental profits, you need to take your gross rental income in the year and subtract any ongoing, property-related expenses. The accounting period for all rental income is the tax year, i.e. April 6 to the following April 5. Each tax year, you should prepare a **Rental Income and Expenditure Account** to establish whether or not you have made a profit. These accounts do not need to be submitted to the Taxman - just keep them for your records and to help you complete the Land and Property pages on your tax return. The spreadsheet lists the various types of expense that you can deduct from your rental income. Basically, any costs that you incur in the day-to-day running of your property investment business can be deducted from your rental income.

RENTAL INCOME AND EXPENDITURE ACCOUNT

	Apr	May	Jun	Jul	Aug	Sep	Oct	Nov	Dec	Jan	Feb	Mar	Total
Rental statement													
Rental income (excluding deposits)													
Expenses:													
Rent, rates, insurance (box 5.24)													
Rent:													
Ground rent													
Service charges													
Rates:													
Water rates													
Council Tax paid on behalf of tenants													
Insurance:													
Buildings													
Contents													
Gas service contract													
Appliance cover													
Other													
Other													
Other													
Repairs, maintenance, renewals (box 5.25)													
Repairs to the property													
Repairs to the fixtures and fittings													
Repairs to windows and doors													
Repairs to the garden area													
Maintenance - gas													
Maintenance - electricity													
Maintenance - plumbing													
Maintenance - internal decorating													
Maintenance - external decorating													
Cost of annual gas safety certificate													
Renewals													
(leave blank if you want to claim the "wear & tear" allowance in box 5.17)													
Finance charges including interest (box 5.26)													
Interest on loans to purchase property													

Legal and professional costs (box 5.27)

	Apr	May	Jun	Jul	Aug	Sep	Oct	Nov	Dec	Jan	Feb	Mar	Total
Costs of agents for letting and collecting rents													
Agents (etc.) charges for preparing inventories													
Legal fees													
Accountants' fees													
Other professional costs													

Services provided including wages (box 5.28)

	Apr	May	Jun	Jul	Aug	Sep	Oct	Nov	Dec	Jan	Feb	Mar	Total
Gardener													
Window cleaner													
Cleaner													
Security													
Wages of those providing services for you													
Cost of house clearances													
Other services provided													
Other services provided													
Other services provided													

Other expenses (box 5.29)

	Apr	May	Jun	Jul	Aug	Sep	Oct	Nov	Dec	Jan	Feb	Mar	Total
Travelling (to and from the property)													
Stationery													
Telephone calls													
Other out of pocket expenses of running the business													
Other expenses													

Total Expenses (box 5.24 to box 5.29)

	Apr	May	Jun	Jul	Aug	Sep	Oct	Nov	Dec	Jan	Feb	Mar	Total

Rental income less expenses

Wear & Tear allowance (box 5.37)
10% of gross rental income less water rates and council tax.
(Can only be claimed if you haven't claimed the cost of renewals in box 5.35)

Net profit (before tax adjustments)

	Apr	May	Jun	Jul	Aug	Sep	Oct	Nov	Dec	Jan	Feb	Mar	Total

Schedule of capital costs

Costs that you incur in the day-to-day running of your property investment business are not capital expenses, and so can be deducted from your rental income. As that just leaves the capital costs, what should you do with them?

IMPROVEMENTS

Costs incurred in significantly improving your property are considered capital and cannot be deducted. But, even though you can't offset these improvement costs against your rental income, you will usually be able to offset them against your capital gain when you sell the property. Keep a record of these costs by updating the **Schedule of Capital Costs** each time you complete your rental accounts and tax return.

SCHEDULE OF CAPITAL COSTS

Property address: . . . . *(insert address)*

Date purchased: . . . . *(insert date)*

Tax year-ended	Total cost of work done on property £	Amount claimed against rental income as repairs £	Amount to add to cost of property £
	Total capital expenditure added to cost of property		

Rental business job description

You can get a tax deduction for paying your spouse/partner a wage for managing a property on your behalf. However, as with all things to do with the Taxman, you have to get the paper trail right.

WAGES OF SPOUSE

As long as they don't own a share in the property, you can pay your spouse or partner a wage for dealing with the administration of your let properties. And this wage can be offset against your rental income. This is a good way for them to receive some income from the property without you having to give them a share in it. Their duties could include finding tenants, arranging inventories, check ins/outs, dealing with tenant queries, preparing the rental accounts - get your partner to sign a **Rental Business Job Description** detailing exactly what their duties will be.

COMMERCIAL REWARD

The Taxman says you have to pay them a "proper commercial reward" for the work they do. For a commercial rate per hour, have a look at what a managing agent would charge you and then discount this by 50% for a non-specialist putting the hours in. However, you mustn't pay less than the National Minimum Wage, currently £5.73 per hour (rising to £5.80 in October 2009). It's likely that a managing agent would charge a fee of at least £15 per hour, so you could pay £7.50.

RENTAL BUSINESS JOB DESCRIPTION

Job title	Property letting administrator
Accountability	Property owner(s)
Location	Home-based and the various properties
Brief description	To run the letting business
Duties and responsibilities	1. Place adverts for tenants
	2. Arrange for inventories to be carried out
	3. Check ins/outs
	4. Dealing with tenant queries
	5. Arrange for repairs to be carried out
	6. Liaise with CORGI registered engineers to carry out the annual gas safety checks
	7. Keep up to date with the health and safety regulations as they apply to property landlords
	8. Carry out property inspections and updating repairs/renewals plan
	9. Rent collection
	10. Chase up overdue rent via telephone and personally
	11. Keep proper records of rental income and expenditure and prepare a monthly rental income and expenditure account
	12. Prepare the year-end rental accounts and complete the Land and Property pages of the self-assessment tax return
Hours of work	Two hours per week (flexible overtime may be required)
Transport	You are expected to use your own car to visit the properties. You will be reimbursed at the HMRC authorised mileage rates which are 40p for the first 10,000 miles and 25p thereafter
Rate of pay	£7.50 per hour

Capital allowances election

More often than not, when a commercial building is sold, the seller, having made a claim for capital allowances, will ask the buyer to enter into a special tax agreement. What format should this take to satisfy the Taxman?

CAPITAL ALLOWANCES

If you own a commercial property (or furnished holiday accommodation), you can't deduct the full cost of any fixtures and fittings that you purchase against the rental income you receive as the fixtures are likely to last for more than one year. Instead, you can usually claim a percentage (normally 25% a year) of their cost. This percentage is known as a capital allowance (CA). Normally this can be done by making a **Capital Allowances Election**, which basically means that the buyer and seller decide between themselves how much of the sale price is allocated to the fixtures and fittings in the building.

AGREED VALUE

There is no legal requirement to agree a value at the tax-written down value (original cost less CAs already claimed by the seller). Whilst this may be of benefit to the seller's tax position, as they won't have to pay tax on any overclaim of allowances, it will be a disadvantage to the buyer. The higher the agreed value for fixtures and fittings, the greater the allowances to the buyer - where the seller's tax rate is lower than the buyer's tax rate, there may be scope for the buyer to negotiate a higher disposal value by meeting the seller's tax clawback. The election must be made in writing within two years of the date of contract of sale and is irrevocable.

CAPITAL ALLOWANCES ELECTION

Notification of an Election to use an alternative apportionment in accordance with s.198 **Capital Allowances Act 2001**, between . . . . *(insert name of seller)* and . . . . *(insert name of buyer)*.

Property address: . . . .

Interest (freehold/leasehold): . . . .

Seller's name and address: . . . .

Tax district and reference: . . . .

Buyer's name and address: . . . .

Tax district and reference: . . . .

Date of completion of sale: . . . .

Amount apportioned to machinery and plant fixtures (£): . . . .

(see attached for details)

Sale price (£): . . . .

The seller and the buyer hereby jointly elect, pursuant to the provisions of s.198 Capital Allowances Act 2001, that the amount of the sale price to be treated as capital expenditure on plant and machinery incurred by the buyer on the provision of the fixtures is . . . . *(insert amount as above)*. A list of the fixtures is given on the next page.

Signed: . . . .

Name of Seller: . . . .

Date: . . . .

Signed: . . . .

Name of Buyer: . . . .

Date: . . . .

Example:

Schedule of Plant and Machinery to included in s.198 Election

. . . .*(insert address)*

Item	Apportioned Amount
Ventilation	£4,500.00
Blinds	£1,500.00
Total	**£6,000.00**

CLAUSES FOR CONTRACT

1. Have any of the Fixtures included in the transaction been included in an election either under s.198 or s.199 Capital Allowances Act 2001 (previously s.59B of the Capital Allowances Act 1990)? If so, please provide a copy of such election notice(s).

2. If requested by us, will you enter into an agreement with us to make an election under s.198 or s.199 of the Capital Allowances Act 2001?

Capital allowances checklist

If you buy an industrial or commercial building - whether to trade from it yourself or let it out - you should be able to claim capital allowances on plant and fixtures that are contained in the building. How do you make sure you don't lose out?

IDENTIFY THE FIXTURES

Capital allowances (CAs) allow the cost of capital assets to be written off against a business's taxable profits. So in this type of situation there are three points to remember: **(1)** the building itself won't generally give you any kind of CA; **(2)** the plant and fixtures in the building probably will give you CAs, so you need to separately identify these; and **(3)** if you don't do this up-front, it's difficult to argue what their value is later on. Indeed, the Taxman is entitled to insist that a *"just and reasonable apportionment"* be made between the building and any plant etc. eligible for CAs. You can bet this won't be biased in your favour, so you need to include a figure in the purchase contract. Use our **Capital Allowances Checklist** to identify and record the fixtures and fittings within a building that qualifies for CAs.

Stamp duty. These allocations are also normally intended to mitigate Stamp Duty Land Tax (SDLT).

CAPITAL ALLOWANCES CHECKLIST

Capital allowances can only be claimed on plant and machinery and not on buildings. However, the legislation specifies those assets that, while falling under the definition of buildings, will qualify as plant. These items are listed separately under their relevant section.

Asset description	Date acquired	Original cost (£)	Capital allowances [already claimed] (£)	Sale value (£)
Electrical systems (specific to trade):				
Wiring to fixed plant				
Switchgear				
Emergency lighting				
Specialised lighting (e.g. window display)				
Other:				
Space and water heating systems				
Hot water system				
Air conditioning (including any associated suspended ceiling or floor)				
Air purification system				
Manufacturing or processing equipment (list):				
Storage equipment (list):				
Cold room				

Asset description	Date acquired	Original cost (£)	Capital allowances [already claimed] (£)	Sale value (£)
Display equipment (list):				
White goods:				
Cooker				
Washing machine				
Dishwasher				
Refrigerator				
Other:				
Sanitary fittings:				
Washbasins				
Sinks				
Baths				
Showers				
Other:				
Networking systems:				
Computer network system (including wiring)				
Telephone network system (including wiring)				
Walkways:				
Lifts				
Hoists				
Escalators				
Moving walkways				

Asset description	Date acquired	Original cost (£)	Capital allowances [already claimed] (£)	Sale value (£)
Fire and security equipment:				
CCTV				
Sound insulation				
Fire alarm system				
Fire extinguishers				
Sprinkler system				
Mechanical door closers				
Other fire-fighting equipment				
Burglar alarm system				
Safe				
Other:				
Fixtures and fittings:				
Moveable partitioning				
Carpets				
Removable floor coverings				
Blinds				
Curtains				
Mezzanine floor				
Trade and information signs				
Any other machinery not listed above:				
TOTAL DISPOSAL VALUE				

Declaration of trust

Many people buy their first investment property in their sole name. However, buying a property jointly can have significant tax savings. But what if you don't want a 50:50 split of the income/profit with your partner?

JOINTLY OWNED PROPERTY

There may be situations where it is preferable for you to own a property jointly with your spouse. For example, you're both basic-rate taxpayers, but if you were the sole owner, the rental income would take you into the higher-rate band. By owning the property jointly, you can both have a share of the rental income and stay below the higher-rate band. The Taxman will automatically treat you and your spouse as sharing the income 50:50 even if you don't actually own the investment in equal shares. This could be a problem where you want to allocate more of the rental profits to the lower earning spouse. However, if you don't own the property in equal proportions, you can jointly elect to be taxed on your actual shares. To do this you must both complete and sign a declaration form, which you can download from http://www.hmrc.gov.uk/forms/form17.pdf and send it to the Taxman. To support this declaration, you need to have evidence that the property is actually owned in unequal proportions by signing a **Declaration of Trust**.

DECLARATION OF TRUST

THIS DECLARATION OF TRUST is made the . . . . . . *(insert day)* day of . . . . . . *(insert month and year)*

BETWEEN

(1) . . . . *(insert your name)*

(2) . . . . *(insert your spouse's name)*

NOW THIS DEED WITNESSES as follows:

1. Percentage holding

It is declared that the property at . . . . *(insert address)* is held in the following percentages:

. . . .   *(insert your name)*   . . . . *(insert percentage holding)*

. . . .   *(insert your spouse's name)*   . . . . *(insert percentage holding)*

2. Mortgage

For as long as there is a mortgage on the property, this deed provides that it be paid off before the sale proceeds are divided in the above percentages.

3. Right of pre-emption

If one party to this trust wishes to sell the property they should first give notice of this intention to the other party who would have the right to buy that person's share at market value.

SIGNED AND DELIVERED AS A DEED by:

. . . .

(insert your name)   *(insert your spouse's name)*

WITNESSED by:

. . . .

(insert witness's name and address)

Property management company contract

When companies have lower effective tax rates than individuals, it might make sense to divert some of your rental income into your own property management company. How can you avoid a challenge from the Taxman on such an obvious way to save tax?

PROPERTY MANAGEMENT COMPANY

Whether to buy a property personally or through a limited company is a common question asked by property investors. Although companies currently have lower effective tax rates (say, 21%) than individuals (say, 40%), there could be a further tax charge when taking money out of the company as salary or dividends. However, by setting up a company to manage your property portfolio, you can take advantage of the lower company tax rates (as some or all of your rental profits will be diverted through the company). The company would provide the usual letting agent services, such as ongoing maintenance, repairs and property inspections and would charge you at a commercial rate for this service. Commercial letting agents usually charge around 15% of the gross rental income for a full management service. Therefore, if you rent out a property for £1,000 a month, then the company can charge you £150 a month (15% of £1,000) as a management fee. The company could also make separate charges for drawing up a tenancy agreement or taking an inventory. To rebuff any challenges from the Taxman, you should have a written **Property Management Company Contract** in place. The contract should outline the management services that the company is providing to you and their related charges.

PROPERTY MANAGEMENT COMPANY CONTRACT

Contract for management services

This agreement is made on . . . . *(insert date of agreement)* between

. . . . *(insert property management company name)* (the "Company") and

. . . . *(insert property owner name)* (the "Property Owner")

Finding tenants

The Company will find a suitable tenant for the Property Owner for a fee of . . . . . . *(insert figure)*. This fee must be paid upon commencement of the tenancy. The service will include: continuously and vigorously advertising the property until it has been let to a suitable tenant. Interviewing and vetting all suitable prospective tenants and taking them to view the property. Taking up references from all tenants and supplying contracts.

Ongoing management service

For . . . . *(insert figure)* of the rental payment over the period of the Tenancy Agreement, the Company will carry out the following services on behalf of the Property Owner:

- rent collection
- notification to service companies at the commencement of the tenancy e.g. gas, electric, water, Council Tax
- arrangement and supervision of minor repairs to the property and general maintenance.

Additional services

Inventory

The Company will charge a fee of . . . . *(insert figure)* for preparing an inventory. This includes compiling an inventory for three bedrooms, two reception areas, kitchen and bedroom. For each additional room or out house there will be an extra charge of £. . . . . . . *(insert figure)*.

Renewal

If the original tenancy is extended for the same tenant or occupier, a further charge will become payable to the Company at the outset of such extended periods at the rate of £ . . . . *(insert figure)* of the rental payable during the extended period.

Inspections

The Company will make quarterly inspections during the period of letting to ensure the premises are being used in an appropriate manner. The charge will be £. . . . *(insert figure)* per inspection.

Signed on behalf of the Company . . . .

Name (in capitals) . . . .

Position . . . .

Signed by the Property Owner . . . .

Date . . . .

Chattels checklist

Anything moveable is generally not considered to be part of a property and so not subject to Stamp Duty Land Tax. How can you safely use this to your advantage?

STAMP DUTY LAND TAX - CHATTELS

You have to pay Stamp Duty Land Tax (SDLT) when you buy a property over a certain price threshold. SDLT is calculated as a percentage of the purchase price of the property and is paid by the purchaser. Between £175,000 and £250,000 SDLT is 1% on residential property until December 31 2009. Once the price passes the £250,000 threshold, the amount of SDLT due jumps to 3%; so as a buyer, you would like to keep the price under £250,000; similarly, when the price jumps to over £500,000 you pay 4%. The seller, on the other hand, doesn't have to pay SDLT, so will want to get as much as possible for their property. The solution would be for both you and the seller to come to an agreement whereby the seller prices the property below £250,000, or £500,000, and you pay separately for any fixtures and fittings (chattels). However, if the Taxman disputes the amount attributed to the chattels, he will request a full inventory and breakdown of the consideration - so use our **Chattels Checklist** to record the value of the relevant items.

CHATTELS CHECKLIST

Chattel	Approximate market value (£)
Inside the property:	
Carpets	
Flooring	
Curtains	
Blinds	
Lamp shades	
Light fittings	
Mirrors	
Coat hooks and stands	
Freestanding kitchen white goods:	
Cooker	
Microwave	
Fridge	
Freezer	
Dishwasher	
Washing machine	
Tumble dryer	
Extractor fan	
Portable appliances:	
Electric fires	
Gas fires	
Fans	
Humidifier	
Other:	
Other:	
Other:	
In the garden:	
Garden shed (and contents)	
Garden ornaments	
Plants in pots	
Flood lights	
Other:	
Other:	

Licence agreement

If you purchase a commercial property personally and then lease it to, say, your company, you could end up paying Stamp Duty Land Tax on the lease. How can you avoid this potential problem?

STAMP DUTY LAND TAX - LICENCE AGREEMENT

Stamp Duty Land Tax (SDLT) is due on the grant of a lease. The amount payable is based on the net present value (NPV), i.e. the value in today's money of all the rent payable under the lease over its full term. Where the NPV exceeds £175,000 (residential, until December 31 2009) or £150,000 (non-residential), SDLT is due at the rate of 1% of the excess. If you let your company occupy a property owned by you personally in return for a rent, the Taxman could argue that you have granted a lease, even where there is no paperwork to prove that you have done so. If he treats it as a lease, then he could seek to collect the overdue SDLT plus interest and penalties. However, this can be avoided by using a **Licence Agreement** instead of a lease. A licence cannot be sold or given away, whereas a lease can be assigned to someone else.

LICENCE AGREEMENT

In respect of . . . . *(insert address)*

THIS LICENCE is made on . . . . *(insert date)*

Between

. . . . *(insert name)*, ("the Licensor") and

. . . . *(insert Company name)*, ("the Licensee")

The Licensor and the Licensee have agreed to occupation of the premises known as . . . . *(insert property address)* on the following terms:

The Licence to run for a term of . . . . . *(insert term length)* commencing on . . . . . *(insert start date)* and expiring on . . . . *(insert finish date)*. At the end of the Licence the Licensee will offer vacant possession if a formal renewal has not been completed.

The Licence fee to be £ . . . . . *(insert figure)* per month, payable in advance calendar monthly by standing order. This fee is exclusive of all non-domestic and water rates and all other outgoings and is payable from . . . . *(insert start date)*.

The Licensor reserves the right to increase or decrease the Licence fee at their discretion. The Licensor will give the Licensee reasonable written notice of any significant increase or decrease in the fees payable.

The Licensee to maintain and give up on termination of the Licence the interior of the premises in as good and substantial repair and decoration as exists before this Licence commences and the Licensee upon notice shall immediately attend to necessary repairs.

The Licensee to comply with any enactments or regulations or such like which may be required from any competent Authority.

The Premises are not to be used other than for normal . . . . . *(insert office / manufacturing, etc.)* purposes in connection with the Licensee's proposed business. The Licensee is not to do or permit anything to be done on the premises which is illegal.

The Licensee to insure and keep insured the premises against loss by fire and such other perils.

The Licensee to permit the Licensor at any reasonable time to enter the premises.

The Licensee to indemnify and keep indemnified the Licensor against all actions, claims and demands arising from the Licensee's use and occupation of the premises.

At any time within the term of the Licence, the Licensee or Licensor may give one calendar month's notice to terminate this Licence.

By signing this agreement, the Licensee formally acknowledges that this is a Licence only and no tenancy is created, whether formal or informal.

Signed for the Licensor: . . . .

Name: . . . . *(insert your name)*

Date: . . . .

Signed for the Licensee: . . . .

Name: . . . . *(insert Company name)*

Date: . . . .

Nominating a residence election

**If you own two or more properties and you haven't told the
Taxman which is your main residence for tax purposes,
he will make the choice that suits him best. What should you do
to fix things in your favour?**

MORE THAN ONE

The general rule is that if you make a gain on the sale of your main residence, then you don't have to pay Capital Gains Tax. An unmarried individual or a married couple can only have one main residence (their principal private residence or PPR) for this relief at any one time.

However, if you've got more than one home, it's possible to nominate which one you would like to be treated as your PPR. By doing this, it's possible to minimise the tax charge on both properties by switching your PPR between them. From the date of acquiring your second property, you have two years to make the **Nominating a Residence Election** and send it to your local tax office. In the case of a married couple, both partners must sign the election for it to be effective.

NOMINATING A RESIDENCE ELECTION

HMRC

. . . . *(insert address)*

. . . .

. . . .

. . . .

. . . . *(insert date)*

Your ref *(insert your ten digit tax reference)*

Dear Sirs

Private residence election

I acquired a second residence on . . . . . . *(insert purchase date)*. In accordance with the provisions of s.222(5) **Taxation of Chargeable Gains Act 1992**, I hereby elect that the following property should be treated as my main residence with effect from . . . . . *(insert date)*:

. . . . *(insert address)*

. . . .

. . . .

. . . .

Please could you acknowledge receipt of this election.

Yours faithfully

. . . . *(insert name)*

Variation of private residence election

As soon as you acquire a second (or even third) residence, you should consider which one you want the Taxman to treat as your principal private residence. Will just a telephone call do?

MORE THAN ONE MAIN RESIDENCE

Once you've nominated a principal private residence (PPR), you can change it by making a **Variation of Private Residence Election** in writing to the Taxman; a telephone call is insufficient. The new election can be backdated by up to two years. As a planning tip, when making the election choose the property that's most likely to make a bigger capital gain or be sold first. If you do end up selling the other one first, then you can simply change the election.

VARIATION OF PRIVATE RESIDENCE ELECTION

HMRC

. . . . *(insert address)*

. . . .

. . . .

. . . .

. . . . *(insert date)*

Your ref . . . . *(insert your ten digit tax reference)*

Dear Sirs

Variation of private residence election

I have currently elected that . . . . . . *(insert address)* should be treated as my main residence for Chargeable Gains Tax purposes. In accordance with the provisions of s.222(5) **Taxation of Chargeable Gains Act 1992**, I now wish . . . . *(insert address)* to be regarded as my main residence with effect from . . . . *(insert date)*.

Please could you acknowledge receipt of this election.

Yours faithfully

. . . . *(insert name)*

Chapter 9

Inheritance Tax

Nil-rate band history

Since Autumn 2007, Inheritance Tax planning between spouses and civil partners has become easier. What are the new provisions and what do you need to be aware of in calculating your tax-free allowance?

NIL-RATE CHANGE

On October 9 2007 the Chancellor announced changes to the rules governing Inheritance Tax (IHT) so that married couples or civil partners could combine their IHT allowances. They can now transfer the tax-free allowance, also referred to as the nil-rate band (NRB), to their spouse/civil partner when they die.

The NRB is currently £325,000 per person, so couples can now protect up to £650,000 of their estate from IHT on the death of the second spouse. This is not a doubling of the tax-free threshold per se, as couples who undertook careful financial planning have always been able to shelter their total tax-free allowance from the Taxman. This was usually done by setting up an NRB trust on the death of the first spouse, but the new rules make this a simpler procedure.

TAX-FREE THRESHOLD

The transferable allowance will be available to all surviving spouses or partners who die from October 9 2007, regardless of when the first spouse died. The tax-free threshold available on death of the second spouse will be equivalent to double the NRB applicable at that time. Gordon Brown has pledged that the NRB will rise to £350,000 in 2010, so if a second spouse dies after April 2010, £700,000 of the state will be free from IHT as long as the first spouse has not used any of their allowance on their death. Each time there is a significant event, for example, if the first spouse leaves money or assets in their will to members of the family or others, this will be deducted from their NRB. Therefore, you'll need to start keeping a record of the **Nil-Rate Band History** to keep track of how much of the NRB remains in place.

NIL-RATE BAND HISTORY

Date of gift (Note 1)	Name and relationship of recipient and description of assets	Value at date of gift (£)	Amount and type of exemption claimed (Note 2)	Net value after exemptions (£)
			Total	

Notes

1. Cheques are gifted on payment (not when cheque is received), i.e. the gift remains incomplete until the cheque is cleared by the paying bank.

2. The following are exempt from IHT:

   (1) Gifts made between spouses.

   (2) Gifts made seven years before death.

   (3) Gifts made out of income other than capital.

   (4) Gifts of up to £250 per person per tax year.

   (5) Gifts to charities, political parties, housing associations and for the benefit the nation (such as works of art to a museum, or properties to the National Trust).

   (6) Gifts on marriage (£5,000 per parent, £2,500 from other relatives and £1,000 from anyone else).

   (7) Up to £3,000 per tax year to a single individual (£6,000 if you haven't used the previous year's allowance).

3. Also record here any unused NRB inherited from your spouse.

Letter of wishes

A discretionary will allows your executors to make decisions according to current tax law, the final assets in the estate and the financial/health circumstances of the beneficiaries. However, there is a way you can specify how you would prefer your estate to be distributed.

IHT PLANNING

In your will you will have appointed executors to manage your estate for the benefit of your spouse/family. The executors will have wide powers, not only in relation to the management of the assets of the trust, but also in relation to the timing and manner in which those assets are distributed. However, you can leave them a **Letter of Wishes** to follow which includes putting in place a particular Inheritance Tax (IHT) planning scheme, e.g. an IOU loan scheme concerning an investment property. As this letter is not legally binding upon the trustees, circumstances may arise under which they consider, quite properly, that to follow it would be inappropriate, i.e. the law changes and the scheme isn't worth implementing.

PERSONAL ITEMS

Apart from major assets such as a house, there may well be relatively minor items to deal with as part of your estate. Let's say you have actually made specific bequests of valuable personal items to beneficiaries in your will. If you change your mind, you will have the expense of then redrafting clauses in your will. Alternatively, you can draft a letter of wishes outlining what you would like to see happen and lay this alongside your will (but not attached to it). Of course, using a letter of wishes (not your will) to make bequests can lead to problems if there is a dispute, because the letter isn't a legally binding document.

The advantage of this for IHT is that your executors might then be able to include these items in household and personal effects (at one third of insurance value) as part of your estate rather than drawing them to the attention of the Capital Taxes Office (CTO) in the will for separate evaluation for IHT. The CTO does not get to see the letter of wishes, only the will!

LETTER OF WISHES

LETTER OF WISHES

Dated . . . . *(insert date)*

To: The Trustees of my Will

By my Will, I have appointed you as my Trustees and have left you the whole or part of my estate to hold in Discretionary Trusts for the benefit of my wife/husband* and family. My Will gives you wide powers not only in relation to the management of the assets of the Trust Fund, but also in relation to the timing and manner in which those assets are distributed.

This letter is not legally binding upon you. Circumstances may arise under which you consider, quite properly, that to follow strictly this letter of wishes would be inappropriate.

1. During the lifetime of my wife/husband*

Whilst my wife/husband* is alive I wish you to regard her/him* as the principal beneficiary, ensuring so far as is possible that her/his* wishes are observed and her/his* welfare regarded as being of paramount importance. Subject to my wife's/husband's* wishes and welfare, I would want you to exercise your powers in such a way as will secure the least amount of tax being payable on my wife's/husband's* death.

2. After the death of my wife/husband*

After the death of the survivor of me and my wife/husband*, I should like you to divide the Trust Fund equally between my children as and when they each attain the age of . . . . *(insert age)*.

Once a child reaches . . . *(insert age)*, I would expect you to distribute her/his* share outright. However, there may be circumstances justifying the postponement of a distribution beyond the age of . . . *(insert age)*, for example, the child may be a party to an unstable marriage, may be embarking on a risky business venture or may wish her/his* share to be retained in Trust for the benefit of her/his* children, thereby mitigating the impact of Inheritance Tax, Income Tax or Capital Gains Tax.

Whilst any of my children are between the age of . . . . *(insert age range)*, I should be quite happy to see the income from their respective shares of the Trust Fund distributed to them.

Death of child

If any of my children should fail to attain the age of . . . *(insert age)*, but have children of their own, then I would expect that my deceased child's share would be retained on Trust for the benefit of his/her* children when they, in turn, reach . . . *(insert age)* and the share treated much in the same way as their deceased parent's share (as mentioned above).

In the event of my wife/husband* and all my children (and any children they may have) dying before the Trust Fund has been fully distributed, then I would expect you to distribute the Trust Fund as follows: . . . . *(insert details of how you would like the Trust Fund distributed).*

I reserve the right to revoke or vary these wishes.

Signed: . . . .

Dated: . . . .

* delete as appropriate

Severing a joint tenancy

Investing in a property jointly can have significant tax savings. However, if one of you dies, your half automatically passes to the other before any will comes into effect. How can you make sure your share goes where you want it to?

AUTOMATIC TRANSFER

Most couples that jointly own a home assume they own half each. This is rarely true. In almost all cases, homes are owned under what is called joint tenancy. This means that if one of you dies, your half automatically passes to the other before any will comes into effect and therefore cannot be considered to be part of your estate. To get around this you must sever the joint tenancy and replace it with a tenancy-in-common. You can use our **Severing a Joint Tenancy** document for first part of this process.

SEVERING A JOINT TENANCY

From: . . . . *(insert name 1)*

Of: . . . . *(insert address)*

To: . . . . *(insert name 2)*

Of: . . . . *(insert address)*

Property: . . . .*(insert property details)*

Title Number: . . . . *(insert title number)*

Notice

I . . . . . . *(insert name 1)*, now give you notice terminating with immediate effect our joint tenancy in the property so that the property will be held by us as tenants-in-common in:

. . . . *(insert details, e.g. the following shares, namely 30% held for you and 70% held for me, or equal shares; shares yet to be decided).*

I request you to acknowledge receipt of this notice by signing and returning the duplicate notice and application enclosed.

Dated: . . . .*(insert date)*

Signed: . . . . *(insert signature of name 1)*

Enc

Receipt of notice

I . . . . . . *(insert name 2)*, now acknowledge receipt of the notice of which this is a copy.

I [do accept/do not accept/make no comment on*] the apportionment of the shares in the beneficial estate described above. I understand that the joint tenancy has been severed.

Dated: . . . .*(insert date)*

Signed: . . . .*(insert signature of name 2)*

* delete as necessary

Application for restriction

We . . . .*(insert name 1 and name 2)* now apply to the Registrar for a restriction to be entered against the title to the property as follows:

"Except under an order of the Registrar or of the court, no disposition by a sole proprietor of the land (not being a trust corporation) under which the capital money arises to be registered."

Dated:. . . . . *(insert date)*

Signed:. . . . . *(insert signature of name 1)*

Dated: . . . .*(insert date)*

Signed: . . . .*(insert signature of name 2)*

Deed of gift

Sometimes it's necessary to transfer a share of your property to someone else in order to make your estate planning arrangements more effective. What simple documentation can you use to effect this?

SHARE YOUR ESTATE

A **Deed of Gift** document can be used, for example, to transfer assets from one spouse to another, *"I gift half of [....] to my spouse in order to formally recognise that they have contributed to the home in other than monetary terms."* Where no money changes hands, a deed of gift is an economical way of effecting the transfer.

Indeed, if the home is currently in one name only, then whoever owns it should make a gift of half of it to the other spouse.

If you are using a deed of gift you will also need a tenancy-in-common declaration to show how the property is now split.

DEED OF GIFT

THIS DEED OF GIFT is made the . . . . . *(insert day)* day of . . . . . *(insert month)* 20[ ]
BETWEEN

. . . .*(insert name)* called the [Donor][Assignor] on the one part
and

. . . .*(insert name)* called the [Donee][Assignee] of the other part
WHEREAS

1. The donor is the beneficial owner of the . . . . . *(insert description of asset)* called the [Asset] [the policy particulars] [of which are contained in the schedule hereto].

2. The donor wishes to transfer the Asset and the full benefit thereof to the donee by way of gift.

NOW THIS DEED WITNESSES as follows

1. In consideration of [the premises] [his/her natural love and affection for the Donee] the Donor as beneficial owner HEREBY [GIFTS][ASSIGNS] the [Asset] for the full benefit thereof and all moneys thereby to become payable under or by virtue thereof to the [Donee][Assignee] by way of gift TO HOLD the same absolutely.

[2. The Assignor covenants with the Assignee that the policy is now valid and in full force.

3. The Assignor shall not be under any obligation whatever to keep up the policy or top reinstate it the same if it shall become void, nor shall the Assignee have any right whatever by way of lien or otherwise reimbursement of any sum or sums paid or provided by the assignor to keep up or reinstate the policy.

4. It is hereby certified that this instrument falls within category L in the Schedule to the **Stamp Duty (Exempt Instruments) Regulations 1987.**]

IN WITNESS whereof the parties hereto have signed this instrument as their deed in the presence of the persons mentioned below the day and year first above written.

[THE SCHEDULE ABOVE REFERED TO IS:

Life office: . . . . *(insert life office)*

Policy number(s): . . . . *(insert policy number)*

Life/lives assured: . . . . *(insert life / lives assured)*]

Signed and delivered by the said [Donor][Assignor]   . . . .

In the presence of: . . . .

Witness: *(insert witness)* . . . .

Address: . . . . *(insert address)*

Occupation: . . . . *(insert occupation)*

Signed and delivered by the said [Donee][Assignee]
In the presence of:
Witness: . . . . *(insert witness)*

Address: . . . . *(insert address)*

Occupation: . . . .*(insert occupation)*

Tenancy-in-common declaration

You may need a tenancy-in-common declaration for a variety of reasons. Use it as evidence to satisfy the Taxman that the property is now actually owned in unequal proportions.

SPLIT TO YOUR NEEDS

A **Tenancy-in-common Declaration** is usually used when you would like to change the proportion of ownership from an automatic 50:50 split under a joint tenancy. Therefore if you sever a joint tenancy you will need to use this document instead. This declaration should also be used if you are using a deed of gift to share out your property for Inheritance Tax reasons - perhaps you would like to give a third to your partner, not previously named on the deeds? Use this declaration to set out the percentage of ownership.

TENANCY-IN-COMMON DECLARATION

THIS DECLARATION OF TRUST is made the . . . . *(insert day)* day of
. . . . *(insert month and year)*

BETWEEN

(1) . . . .*(insert your name)*

(2) . . . . *(insert your spouse's name)*

NOW THIS DEED WITNESSES as follows:

1. Percentage holding

It is declared that the property at . . . . *(insert address)* is held in
the following percentages:

. . . . (insert your name)   . . . . (insert percentage holding)

. . . . *(insert your spouse's name)* . . . . *(insert percentage holding)*

[2. Mortgage

For as long as there is a mortgage on the property, this deed provides that it be paid off
before the sale proceeds are divided in the above percentages.]

3. Right of pre-emption

If one party to this trust wishes to sell the property they should first give notice of this
intention to the other party who would have the right to buy that person's share at
market value.

SIGNED AND DELIVERED AS A DEED by:

. . . .

(insert your name)   *(insert your spouse's name)*

WITNESSED by: SIGNED by:

. . . .

(insert witness's name)   *(insert witness's signature and address)*

Deed of variation

It's nice to be remembered in a will but this can leave you with an Inheritance Tax problem of your own. Could you vary the terms of the original will so that the bequest passes directly to someone else instead?

NEXT GENERATION

A gift (known as a disposition) made by a deceased person may be disclaimed or varied, e.g. passed on to the next generation, within two years from the date of death. You can use our **Deed of Variation**, to be signed in the presence of a witness, to achieve this. The deed needs to be signed by all the beneficiaries of the will affected by the change.

DEED OF VARIATION

THIS DEED OF VARIATION dated . . . . *(insert date)* made between:

1. "the Executors" . . . . *(insert names)* . . . . *(insert addresses)*

2. "the original Beneficiary" . . . . *(insert name)*

3. "the substituted Beneficiary" . . . . *(insert name)* . . . . *(insert address)*

WHEREAS

    1.1. XY ("the Deceased") died on . . . . . *(insert date)* having made his/her Will ("the Will") on . . . . . *(insert date)* and probate of the Will was granted to the Executors by the District Probate Registry on . . . . . *(insert date)*.

    1.2. AB ("the original Beneficiary") was entitled to . . . . . from the deceased's estate.

2. The original Beneficiary and the substituted Beneficiary:

    2.1. agree that the provisions of the Schedule shall be construed as if they constituted the deceased's will and his/her estate shall be administered accordingly.

    2.2. direct the Executors to distribute the estate of the deceased in accordance with the provisions of the Schedule.

3. The parties elect for section 142 of the **Inheritance Tax Act 1984** and section 62 of the **Taxation of Chargeable Gains Act 1992** to apply to this deed.

4. It is certified that this instrument falls within category M in the schedule to the **Stamp Duty (Exempt Instruments) Regulations 1987**.

SCHEDULE

Signed as a Deed by the Executors in the presence of . . . . *(insert name)*

. . . . *(insert address)*

Signed as a Deed by the Original Beneficiary in the presence of . . . . *(insert name)*

. . . . *(insert address)*

Signed as a Deed by the substituted Beneficiary in the presence of . . . . *(insert name)*

. . . . *(insert address)*

Surplus income record

**There is a legal exemption which excludes from Inheritance Tax,
monetary gifts made out of your surplus income before death.
How do the executors of your estate prove this surplus income tag
after you've gone?**

GIFTS FROM INCOME

There is no financial ceiling or percentage restriction which might otherwise limit the amount you could give away. Any money expended on gifts out of surplus income is in addition to the annual exempt amount of £3,000.

If you decide to go down this route, you should make a record of your income and outgoings in sufficient detail to evidence the surplus income. Complete our **Surplus Income Record** each tax year so that the executors will be able to rebuff any challenge from the Taxman over gifts made out of your income. (Keep this with your will and record of gifts.)

SURPLUS INCOME RECORD

	TAX YEAR (April 5 to April 6)						
	1 2008/9 £	2 2009/10 £	3 20010/11 £	4 2011/12 £	5 2012/13 £	6 2013/14 £	7 2014/15 £
Income							
Salary							
Pension							
Tax credits							
Dividends							
Rent (less expenses)							
Interest							
Other investment income (specify)							
Other income							
Total income							
Expenditure							
Bills							
Expenses							
Nursing home fees							
Medical insurance							
Tax paid							
Other expenditure							
Total expenditure							
Surplus of income over expenditure							
Regular gifts (specify) e.g. cash to son	1,000	1,000	1,000	1,000	1,000	1,000	1,000
Surplus after gifts							

Record of gifts

One weapon in the battle to minimise Inheritance Tax bills is to simply give away as much as possible while you are still alive. Indeed there is even an annual tax exemption to encourage you to do just this. However, if the Taxman ever queries a particular gift (large or small) or series of gifts, how will your executors ward off this challenge?

KEEP A RECORD

If you decide to go down this route, keep a **Record of Gifts** detailing dates, amounts and beneficiaries. Keep your records with your will and update them annually - perhaps a good time to do so is when you complete your tax return. There is no need to tell the Taxman what you've done. It'll be up to your executors to submit the details when dealing with your estate. Retaining supporting evidence of your income e.g. copies of tax returns, and outgoings, e.g. bank statements would also help your executors.

RECORD OF GIFTS

Date of gift (Note 1)	Name and relationship of recipient and description of assets	Value at date of gift (£)	Amount and type of exemption claimed (Note 2)	Net value after exemptions (£)
			Total	

Notes

1. Cheques are gifted on payment (not when cheque is received), i.e. the gift remains incomplete until the cheque is cleared by the paying bank.

2. The following are exempt from IHT:

(1) Gifts made between spouses.

(2) Gifts made seven years before death.

(3) Gifts made out of income other than capital.

(4) Gifts of up to £250 per person per tax year.

(5) Gifts to charities, political parties, housing associations and for the benefit the nation (such as works of art to a museum, or properties to the National Trust).

(6) Gifts on marriage (£5,000 per parent, £2,500 from other relatives and £1,000 from anyone else).

(7) Up to £3,000 per tax year to a single individual (£6,000 if you haven't used the previous year's allowance).

Chattel lease

In order for a gift to be effective for Inheritance Tax purposes, you must be excluded from "benefiting", other than to a limited extent, from the property once you've given it away. However, what would happen if you were to lease it back in some way?

NOT A GIFT WITH RESERVATION

If you officially pass some valuable antiques on to the next generation but keep these objects in your own home, they would still be subject to IHT treatment. And, similarly, all the time that such a benefit exists, the value of a property remains subject to Inheritance Tax (IHT) on your death. So you can't give away a property and still have possession of it. Or can you?

The payment of a market rent/fee normally avoids this so-called gift with reservation problem for IHT. However, the figure should be established by agreement, see our **Chattel Lease**, between two valuers acting for the two sides. To ratify the agreement the rent/fee must, of course, actually be paid.

CHATTEL LEASE

THIS AGREEMENT is made on . . . . *(insert date)*

BETWEEN

(1) . . . .*(insert name of Parents')* ("the Parents"); and

(2). . . . .*(insert name of Children)* (the "Children").

THE BACKGROUND

The Children are the beneficial owners of the chattels set out in the Schedule below (the "Chattels")

The Children wish to allow the Parents the use and enjoyment of the Chattels on the basis of full consideration payable by the Parents.

THE AGREEMENT

1. Bailment

The Children grant a lease of the Chattels to the Parents for the following term and generally on the terms and conditions following:

2. The term

The term of the lease shall be equal to the joint lives and life of the survivor of the Parents, terminable either:

2.1. Upon six months' written notice given by either party

2.2. Immediately upon default of any obligations contained in Clause 9

2.3. Immediately upon both the Parents or the survivor of them becoming mentally incapable within the meaning of s. 94 (2) of the **Mental Health Act 1983**.

3. Ownership

3.1. The Children retain the ownership of the Chattels

3.2. The Children reserve the right to fix any plating or other means of identification to the Chattels

3.3. The Parents covenant not (nor take steps) to sell, deal, charge or part with the Chattels in any other way contrary to the ownership of the Children

3.4. The Parents will immediately pay any sum required to remove any lien which may arise over the Chattels.

4. Enjoyment and housing

4.1. The Children covenant with the Parents (provided the Parents pay the rent and perform the Parents' covenants) that the parents shall peaceably hold and enjoy the Chattels during the term without any interruption by the Children or any person rightfully claiming under or in trust of any of them

4.2. The Chattels shall be housed at . . . . *(insert name of property)* or at other locations from time to time agreed between the Parents and the Children.

5. Rental

5.1. The initial annual rental for the Chattels shall be £. . . . *(insert figure)* per annum (which is agreed by the Children and the Parents to reflect the current open market rental value of the Chattels)

5.2. The rental shall be paid annually; the first year's rental is due on the signing of this agreement (and the Children acknowledge receipt of it); further annual rental payments shall be due on the anniversaries of this agreement.

5.3. The rental shall be reviewable by agreement at three yearly intervals from the date of this Agreement to ensure that the Parents give full consideration for the use and enjoyment of the Chattels. In default of agreement, the reviewed rent shall be determined by a valuer appointed by the President for the time being of the Incorporated Society of Valuers and Auctioneers acting as expert and not an arbitrator, either party shall be at liberty to request the President to make such an appointment.

6. Insurance

6.1. The Parents will insure the Chattels for their full replacement cost comprehensively against all risk with the interest of the Children noted on the Policy and will duly and punctually pay all premiums and on request will promptly produce the insurance policy and proof of payment of premiums to the Children. All claims under such insurance policy will be dealt with in accordance with the written direction of the Children. All claims and moneys received by the Parents under such insurance policy shall be held by the Parents in trust for the Children.

7. Preservation and Repair

7.1. The Parents undertake to preserve the Chattels

7.2. The Parents undertake to keep the Chattels clean and in good and substantial repair and will bear the cost of any repairs not covered by insurance

7.3. The Parents will permit the Children and any person authorised by them at any reasonable hour to view or survey the state and condition of the Chattels

7.4. The Parents will forthwith after being required to do so by the Children make good any want of repair in the Chattels.

Provided that nothing in this clause shall require the Parents to maintain the Chattels in anything other than their current condition or require the Parents to improve or put the Chattels into first rate condition.

8. Security

8.1. The Parents undertake to put in place, maintain and bear the cost of such security arrangements as are from time to time agreed between the Parents and Children or as are reasonably stipulated by the Children to reflect the requirements of any relevant insurance company, advice from the Police or advice otherwise specifically received from a specialist security company engaged for the purpose.

9. Default

If the Parents default in the punctual payment of any of the instalments of rent provided for, or default in the payment of the insurance premiums as provided for, or default in the performance of any of the terms and conditions of this agreement, the Children may immediately retake possession of the Chattels, without notice to the Parents, with or without legal process, and the parents by this agreement authorise and empower the Children to enter the premises or other places where the Chattels may be found to take and carry away the Chattels. All moneys due under this agreement shall become immediately due and payable plus all reasonable costs of repossession.

EXECUTED ON . . . . *(insert date)*

. . . . *(insert signature)*

Loan waiver deed

If you lend someone money and then it is waived, you can get this amount reduced from your estate for Inheritance Tax purposes. How can you achieve this?

REDUCE YOUR ESTATE

Where a loan is made between individuals, e.g. parent to child, the Capital Taxes Office will not accept that it has been waived and the estate of the lender reduced, unless the waiver is effected by deed. Use our **Loan Waiver Deed** to show the Taxman that you don't wish this amount to be taken into consideration when calculating the value of your estate.

LOAN WAIVER DEED

THIS DEED is made by:

(1) "Father" . . . . *(insert name)* of . . . . *(insert address)*

(2) "Son" . . . . *(insert name)* of . . . . *(insert address)*

Recitals

A. Son is indebted to Father for the loan, brief details of which are set out in the schedule below ("the Loan").

B. By this waiver Father intends to utilise the annual exemption available to him under s.19 of **Inheritance Tax Act 1984**.

Waiver

1. Father waives and releases in favour of Son Three Thousand pounds (£3,000) of the Loan.

2. The continuing balance of the indebtedness due under the Loan following this waiver is set out in part 2 of the schedule.

The Schedule

Part 1 - . . . . *(insert details of the Loan)*

Part 2 - balance now . . . . *(insert amount)*

EXECUTED AS A DEED

and DELIVERED on . . . .

FATHER delivered

in the presence of . . . .

Note: *"Father" can be replaced with "Mother"*

"Son" can be replaced with "Daughter"

Lottery syndicate agreement

Are you in a lottery syndicate? Did you know that any winnings (football pools, National Lottery etc.) by the syndicate leader are potentially chargeable to Inheritance Tax as part of their estate? So what do you need to put in place before the big win?

PROTECT THE SYNDICATE LEADER

The good news is that as long as a simple agreement is in existence (and drawn up before the big win!) any winnings by the syndicate are not chargeable to Inheritance Tax as part of the leader's estate. The prior agreement can be verbal or written but we recommend that a written record is made, such as our **Lottery Syndicate Agreement**. (It's not necessary to lodge this with the Capital Taxes Office.)

LOTTERY SYNDICATE AGREEMENT

We, the parties hereunder, contributing (equal) amounts on a weekly/monthly/yearly * basis to the syndicate hereby confirm that the winnings from such a game of chance will be distributed in equal/proportionate * shares to the stake contributed by each individual member as shown below/in the accompanying schedule *. Such stakes/ contributions applied in the purchase of such tickets or the innings arising therefrom and distributed by the appointed manager in accordance with the agreed shares shall not be a gift within **Inheritance Taxes Act 1984** section 2, but shall be treated as having no liability to inheritance tax in accordance with HMRC Statement of Practice E14. The above shall apply to the members of this syndicate including the appointed manager being the first member named below:

Syndicate member	Stake/contribution	% share of prize	Date
(1) Lisa Woods	£1 a week/month/year	50%	July 23 2009
(Signed)			
(Address)			
(2) Penny Sand	£1 a week/month/year	50%	July 23 2009
(Signed)			
(Address)			

(*) Delete as appropriate

Trading status report

Business property relief is available on shares in unquoted companies if certain conditions are met. This means 100% of the market value of those shares will escape Inheritance Tax. However, the Taxman can take this relief away if he can identify "non-trading activities" in the company. How should you set about persuading him otherwise?

NEEDED FOR THE BUSINESS

Business property relief (BPR) will be reduced if the value of the shares reflects any so-called excepted assets held by the company. An asset would be excepted if it had not been used wholly or mainly for business purposes in the previous two years, or if it were not required for future use in the business. For example, if a company has too much cash, the Capital Taxes Office will try to reduce the BPR available on its shares. If you could prove the cash balance was needed for the business, then this would come back into the 100% relief.

Use our **Trading Status Report** board minutes to make it clear to the Taxman why BPR should still apply to these shares.

TRADING STATUS REPORT

Company: .... *(insert company name)*

Period covered by this report .... *(insert period covered)*

Reason for this report

The directors of . . . . . . *(insert company name)* were asked by the Company's tax advisors to consider whether there was any uncertainty about the Company's status as a trading company. Specifically [(for Inheritance Tax business property relief purposes) whether the company's activities were wholly or mainly trading*] or [(for Capital Gains Tax purposes) whether or not non-trading activities were substantial*]. In reaching their conclusion a number of factors were considered (using guidance in Tax Bulletins 53 and 63, and the cases of Farmer v CIR (1999) and CIR v George (2004)) by the directors. These were as follows:

1. Turnover

(For example: "The Company owns an investment property. The receipts from the letting are not substantial* in comparison to its combined trading and letting receipts. On this measure in isolation, the company is a trading company.)

2. The asset base of the company

The value . . . . . *(insert figure)* of the Company's non-trading assets . . . . *(specify, e.g. investment property, surplus cash)* is not significant* in comparison with its total assets . . . . . *(insert figure)*. Again, this basis alone points to the Company being a trading company. [Retention of . . . . . *(insert description of the asset)* previously used for the purposes of the trade was still considered to be a trading activity by the directors.] [The directors also considered it appropriate to take into account intangible assets not shown on the balance sheet when arriving at a figure for the company's total assets. For example, a figure for . . . . *(insert description of intangible asset, e.g. goodwill)* of . . . . . *(insert figure)* has been added to the Company's balance sheet for the purposes of this exercise.] [The directors also considered it appropriate to use the current market values rather than book values of other assets . . . . . *(specify assets)*].

[What appeared to be excessive cash balances are no longer a concern when the other balance sheet assets have been shown at their current market values. This of course includes intangible fixed assets such as goodwill, which did not appear in the balance sheet of the original financial statements of the Company.] [The directors also noted that the cash represents undrawn trading profits, which could have been paid out as salary or dividends in previous years; not the sale proceeds from the sale of an investment which had not been taken out of the company.]

[Although the Company has not satisfied the total assets test it does so on the turnover and employee time tests. It can be argued therefore that the company's cash reserves can be disregarded.]

3. Expenses incurred/time spent by the officers and employees of the Company

On average only . . . . . *(insert figure)* of the Company's total expenses have been incurred on non-trading activities. This proportion is not substantial*.

The company has not and does not devote a substantial* amount of its staff resources, measured by time or in costs incurred, to non-trading activities.

4. The Company's history

The company's history is relevant to any discussion on trading status. (For example, we noted in reviewing the company's accounts that in . . . . *(specify accounting period)* certain receipts were substantial* to total receipts, but if looked at on a longer timescale, they may not be substantial* compared to other receipts over a longer period. Looked at in this context, therefore, the directors are able to conclude that the Company was a trading company over the period . . . . *(specify from when to when)*, even though that period included particular points in time when . . . . . *(describe measure e.g. non-trade receipts)* amounted to a substantial* proportion of total . . . . . . *(describe measure e.g. total receipts)*.

Conclusion

[Some indicators point in one direction and others the opposite way]. We have weighed up the impact of each measure and using the history of the company over . . . . . . *(specify the period e.g. the last five years)* as the overriding context, ... *(specify the period e.g. of the last five years)* confirm that there is no uncertainty about the trading status of the company.

. . . .*(insert signature)*

. . . .*(insert position in the company)*

. . . .*(insert date)*

Note
* *Depending on which tax then substantial means; (1) over 50% (i.e. wholly and mainly) for Inheritance Tax business property relief; or (2) 20% and over for Capital Gains Tax business asset taper relief.*

Option to buy/sell shares clause

In the event of the untimely death of one of the shareholder directors, the surviving shareholders don't want share ownership to go to someone they'd rather not be in business with. You'll need to set this condition down in writing as soon as possible. However, if you don't get the wording right, the outgoing director's estate could end up with an unexpected tax bill. What do you need to change?

SHAREHOLDERS' AGREEMENT

If there is already a shareholders' agreement, you can insert standard clauses which say that, in the event of a shareholder director dying, their personal representatives are obliged to sell and the other shareholders are obliged to buy, the deceased's shares. The price will be fixed by a specified formula, presided over by the company's auditor in case of a dispute.

The Taxman's prevailing view of this is that it represents a binding contract for the sale of the property (shares) in question at the time of the transferor's death. This means that 100% business property relief (BPR) from Inheritance Tax is not available on the deceased's shares. This interpretation of the legislation has not yet been ratified by the courts (no case has been brought) so you could take him on. However, it's not worth incurring the costs because there's a much simpler solution. Grant buy and sell options instead. Because an option for tax purposes doesn't exist when it is granted but when it is exercised, it can't be held to be an existing binding contract.

Make sure you have an up-to-date shareholders' agreement in place with an **Option to Buy/Sell Shares Clause**. This should: **(1)** grant the personal representatives of the deceased shareholder an "option to sell" shares; and **(2)** grant the surviving shareholders an "option to buy" shares. This "option" argument would also work for partnership interests.

OPTION TO BUY/SELL SHARES CLAUSE

Transfer of shares

1. A shareholder shall give notice in writing (hereinafter called "the transfer notice") to the Company that they desire to transfer their share(s). Such notice shall grant an option for the Company to act as their agent for the sale of the share to the Company, or in the event of the Company not opting to purchase, to any member of the Company, or in the event of any share not being taken up, to any person selected by the Directors as one whom it is desirable in the interests of the Company to admit to membership at the fair value to be fixed by the Auditor for the time being of the Company.

2. If the Company, within the space of 56 days after being served with such transfer notice, shall elect to purchase, or shall find a member or persons selected as aforesaid willing to purchase the share (hereinafter called "the purchaser"), and give notice thereof to the proposing transferor, they shall be bound upon payment of the fair value, to transfer the share to the Company or to the purchaser who shall be bound to complete the purchase within 14 days from the service of such last-mentioned notice.

3. The executors or administrators of any deceased member shall have an option, at any time after the expiration of six months from the date of death, if and when called upon by the Directors so to do, to grant an option to buy all the shares registered in the name of the deceased member at the date of their death, or such of the same as still remain so registered, and should such executors or administrators fail to give such transfer notice within a period of 14 days after being so called upon, or should there be no such executors or administrators at the expiration of such period of six months, a transfer notice shall be deemed to have been given.

Chapter 10

Dealings with the Taxman

Self-employed pages review

Before filing a tax return it's a good idea to carry out last minute health checks with a view to reducing the chance of it being selected for an enquiry. This is especially important if you are self-employed. How can you check that your answers won't raise suspicion?

CHECK YOUR ANSWERS

Before submitting any return you should compare all your answers with a copy of last year's return. Satisfy yourself that you can explain any variances in the figures and if these are substantial, write an explanation in the "additional information" box (otherwise known as the white space).

In particular, if you have any self-employed income, it's likely you will need to fill in supplementary pages and include them with your main personal tax return. Checking your answers are consistent with last year's is a good place to start as the Taxman's pre-enquiry screening techniques pick up on any variances. And, use the questions in our **Self-employed Pages Review** to reduce the chances of being selected for an enquiry.

SELF-EMPLOYED PAGES REVIEW

Section of self-employed pages	Actioned
Business details Are the name and description of the business the same as on last year's return? Does the accounting period follow on from last year's return?	
Capital allowances summary Have you claimed capital allowances for fixed assets used in your business? Note. If there is a private use of an asset then the figure you claim for capital allowances must be reduced for this before being entered on the form (e.g. 20% private use would mean only 80% of the figure goes on the return).	
Turnover below £15,000 If your turnover is significantly different from last year then put an explanation in the additional information box. Remember to add your capital allowances to your expenditure figure. Check that your ratio of profit to turnover is consistent with last year. If it is higher check that you have not left any expenses out. If it is lower consider making an additional disclosure as to why it has changed. Note. If your turnover has been just under £15,000 for the last two years this could trigger an enquiry. If it has been, then consider using the detailed boxes in the over £15,000 section instead.	
Income and expenses You are expected to translate your accounts into entries for boxes in this section. There are probably fewer headings on the Taxman's return than are used in your accounts. So you'll need to amalgamate some figures together. For example, there is no separate heading for telephone expenses which means you will have to include them under the catch-all category of "General administrative expenses" (which you should use instead of other expenses as much as possible). It's a good idea to annotate a copy of the detailed profit and loss account (from your self employed accounts) with the box numbers you have used for each income and expense heading, and keep this with your copy of the finished tax return. Indeed, are the expenses claimed in the same boxes as last year's return?	

Section of self-employed pages	Actioned
Income and expenses (cont.)	
Has there been a big increase in the ratio of your purchases to sales, which needs explaining in the additional information box?	
Tax adjustments	
The Taxman will expect to see some disallowed expenses. In particular:	
Has an amount for entertainment been disallowed?	
Has a private use element of expenses been disallowed e.g. an element of both telephone costs and motor expenses?	
Has depreciation been disallowed?	
Have you claimed for capital allowances in both places on the SE pages (Box 3.22 and Box 3.70)?	
Adjustments to arrive at taxable profits	
If you had an overlap relief figure (Boxes 3.78 to 3.80) on last year's return make sure you enter it this year as well.	
Class 4 NI	
Check that (as one of the answers to question 18 on the main tax return) any Class 4 NI which is payable has been entered in Box 18.2B.	
Sub-contractors in the construction industry	
If relevant, remember to enter in Box 3.97 the total amount of tax deducted by contractors shown on the CIS certificates that you have.	
Note. Staple these certificates (having photocopied them first) to this SE page.	
Summary balance sheet	
If you do decide to enter balance sheet figures on SE 4 (although it's not compulsory) ask yourself if the drawings figure (in the capital account) is reasonable and consistent with your living standards and past year's figures.	
Overall	
Compare all your answers with a copy of last year's return. Satisfy yourself that you can explain any variances in the figures and if these are substantial write an explanation in the additional information box (otherwise known as the white space) on page SE4.	
If the variations are because of a change of year-end, cessation or commencement then provide full details of the event and any calculations that arose as a result.	

Section of self-employed pages	Actioned
Overall (cont.)	
Note. The additional information box will only be read if your case is being considered for enquiry. That's when what you record there could deselect you from further enquiry.	
Last resort!	
If you feel that the Taxman couldn't answer his own questions without looking at a set of your self-employed accounts consider sending in a set with the tax return. This way you could reduce your chances of an enquiry being opened just to get at what the accounts show. But only do this as a last resort!	

Out of time letter

Your involvement in an enquiry usually begins when you receive a letter saying that you are the subject of one and asking you to send further information. However, before you reply there is something you ought to check out.

DELIVERED TOO LATE

The statutory requirement is that a notice of enquiry must be given, i.e. received by the taxpayer within the time allowed. For example, with income tax the Taxman has to issue a notice by the anniversary of the January 31 following the end of the tax year. There is a presumption that a notice will be delivered in the ordinary course of post; but this is a rebuttable presumption. What matters is when the notice is actually delivered. If you can show that the notice was delivered after the deadline, it matters not one jot when it was posted; use our **Out of Time Letter** to politely have the enquiry set aside.

OUT OF TIME LETTER

HMRC

. . . . *(insert address)*

. . . .

. . . .

. . . .

. . . . *(insert date)*

Dear . . . .*(insert name)*

Enquiry notice out of time

. . . .***(insert name and tax reference)***

Thank you for your enquiry notification dated . . . .*(insert date)*.

Unfortunately I/we cannot respond to this as the notice itself was delivered outside the time limit for opening such enquiries.

[You can see from the attached photocopy that your notice was date stamped as received by me/us after the deadline for delivering such a notice]

If you have any queries please do not hesitate to contact me/us.

Yours sincerely

. . . .*(insert name)*

. . . .*(insert company name)*

Enc

No interview letter

There is no statutory obligation to attend an interview with the Taxman and some advisors advocate non-attendance. However, how can you persuade your particular tax inspector that this isn't a good idea at this time?

PROBING QUESTIONS

Once they have been through your records, the tax inspector dealing with your enquiry likes to sit down with you and go through a pre-prepared list of questions. He will have already anticipated your answers to some of these and will have more probing follow-up questions to match. The risk at interview is that you might give too much away or just give the wrong answer, all in an attempt to be helpful and get rid of the problem. Therefore, if you don't want to attend an interview, try sending our **No Interview Letter** to the tax inspector dealing with your enquiry.

NO INTERVIEW LETTER

HMRC

. . . . *(insert address)*

. . . .

. . . .

. . . . *(insert date)*

Dear Sirs

. . . .*(insert your business name and tax reference)*

Thank you for your letter dated . . . . *(insert date)* requesting an interview.

It seems clear that I/we have made no attempt to conceal any income or to overstate any expenditure.

If your review of my/our records has thrown up any matters that appear to you prima facie to be unsatisfactory, there appears to be no reason why such matters cannot be aired in writing. I/we have every confidence that a fully acceptable explanation will be available. Nor do I/we think that there are any areas that you would wish to discuss at a meeting but that could not equally be discussed in correspondence.

Moreover, this enquiry has already involved me/us in a great deal of unnecessary expense, and attendance at a meeting would not only add to this expense but could also result in a fairly considerable loss of income.

If, therefore, there are any relevant matters on which you would like additional information, I/we should be pleased if you would specify them, and we will continue to do all I/we can towards bringing this enquiry to an end in the shortest possible time.

In the absence of any suggestion of wrongdoing, however, and for the reasons given above, I/we do not feel that our interests would be best served by interrupting my/our working procedures in order to attend a meeting.

It should also be pointed out that it is not always true to say that "meetings are far more cost-effective and far less time-consuming than dealing with matters by correspondence". Questions of detail might well be impossible to answer from memory across the desk, so that I/we would still have to go away, look up the points, and reply in writing.

Yours faithfully

What the Taxman's likely to ask

The Taxman has a pretty standard set of questions he'll ask at interview. These are mostly designed to undermine the records you've kept and so allow him to make a demand for tax on missing income/ profits or over-claimed expenses. So how should you prepare for such an interview?

GUIDELINES

If you attend an interview, the Taxman should start by explaining that he will ask questions and take notes on your answers. It's best to answer all questions truthfully but not to elaborate. If the inspector wants the detail he can ask. Use our guide to **What the Taxman's Likely to Ask** to help prepare for your interview.

WHAT THE TAXMAN'S LIKELY TO ASK

The business

The Taxman will know the trade (e.g. taxi driver, public house) but he does not know the particular facets of your business (e.g. for a pub is food sold or is it largely beer sales?). The purpose of the questioning will be to try and ascertain a picture of the trade carried on. Remember, you know far more about the business than he does.

Record-keeping

The Taxman will generally, after the interview, ask to have all the business records for review. He needs, therefore, to understand your record-keeping and will ask such questions as: What books are maintained? Who writes them up? How often is this done?

Your accountant's work

Next to be reviewed will be the work undertaken by your accountant. He will want to know, if not covered in the opening letter, which estimates were used. What balance was necessary to square the cash account and how the accountant dealt with that. He will also cover the adjustments necessary to arrive at taxable profit from the profit shown in your accounts, e.g. an adjustment for private use of a motor vehicle.

Drawings and private expenditure

In order that the Taxman can confirm whether the profits are sufficient to meet the capital expenditure and personal and private expenditure, he will review the drawings from the business and your personal needs. He will want to know what is spent in cash e.g. housekeeping, private spending, whether holidays have been taken and whether you have any hobbies i.e. what do you spend your money on?

Assets

If the Taxman has not asked you to complete a Statement of Assets, he will try to establish the investments held and assets purchased. What did it cost? How much of it was financed? Do you have an outstanding loan balance? Have you lent monies to family and friends that haven't been repaid? Have you extended your home? What did it cost and how was it financed?

Other monies received

Do you gamble? Have sums been received by way of a loan? Any legacies? This is to stop the items being offered as excuses once the extent of any understatement of income has been calculated.

Changing interview notes

If you attend an enquiry interview, the Taxman will make his own notes of what he "thinks" was said and use them against you if he can. He will probably try and get you to sign them as a true record of what came up at the meeting. Should you?

READ THE NOTES

Never sign notes at a meeting. Gain yourself some thinking time by saying you would like to go over the notes in some detail. Ask the Taxman to send them to you. Go through the notes looking for all the things that are wrong, both where they do not reflect what was said and where they do but you have since discovered that what was said was incorrect. The latter is one way of changing your mind after the event, particularly if an off-the-cuff remark is not confirmed by what you find in your records. Always make changes to his notes to make them more ambiguous. Even when you send the amended notes back to the Taxman, don't sign but do include our **Changing Interview Notes** covering letter. If the Taxman objects to your refusal to sign the notes, point out to him that the Special Compliance Office (heavy mob) doesn't insist, so why should he!

CHANGING INTERVIEW NOTES

. . . . *(insert name)*

HMRC

. . . . :. . . . . . . *(insert address)*

. . . .

. . . .

. . . .

. . . . *(insert date)*

Dear . . . . *(insert name)*

. . . . ***(insert name and tax reference)***

Thank you for your letter dated . . . . *(insert date)* containing your notes from our meeting held on . . . .*(insert date)*.

I/we have been through the notes looking for items where they do not reflect what we recollect as being said and/or where they do but I/we have since discovered that what was said was incorrect (for example an off the cuff remark has not been confirmed by what I/we you found in our records).

In particular (e.g. the adjustments agreed to at the interview which appear to be too high are . . . .)

I/we have annotated the enclosed copy of the notes accordingly.

However, we are unable to sign the interview notes in accordance with the best practice established following the Wall v IRC case. I/we trust you will not object to this as it is our understanding that not even the Special Compliance Office insist on interview notes being signed.

Yours sincerely

. . . . *(insert signature)*

Checklist for attacking a business economics exercise

In the pursuit of tax collection targets there is now a much greater willingness by the Taxman to displace the profits shown by your accounts with an estimate based on a simple business economics exercise. How do you fight back in these circumstances?

MISSING INCOME?

A typical example of a business economics exercise would be for the Taxman to use a mark-up of purchases to selling price and construct an anticipated sales figure. The next stage is to compare that with the sales shown in the accounts. The difference is, in his view, missing income! The scope for inaccuracies in such an exercise is vast so the Taxman's calculations need to be attacked, not only in terms of the detailed figures employed, but also of the overall credibility of the ratios used, e.g. gross profit percentage.

ATTACK HIS ARGUMENT

So how do you handle the Taxman? Firstly, you have to get hold of his calculations. Write and say that you recognise he has done a lot of work and research to arrive at his reconstruction results. However, could he kindly provide details of his calculations? From here you can start to pick holes in his argument line by line, not accepting any assumption. Use our **Checklist for Attacking a Business Economics Exercise** (or reconstruction as it is sometimes known).

CHECKLIST FOR ATTACKING A
BUSINESS ECONOMICS EXERCISE

The Taxman's calculations	Actioned
Write to the Taxman and say that you recognise he has done a lot of work and research to arrive at his reconstruction results. However, could he kindly provide details of his calculations.	
If one exists for your business make sure you have a copy of the Taxman's "business economics" data. (Visit his website http://www.hmrc.gov.uk/bens to find out)	
Once received, check all the calculations the Taxman provides, line by line. Are they mathematically correct?	
Representative period?	
Is the period chosen by the Taxman in his calculations truly representative of the business' trading year? Check that it excludes, say, exceptionally busy or quiet periods.	
Product mix	
Does the business sell more than one item? If yes, then establish the product mix, i.e. the range of products sold and in what proportion. Do this for a sample period, e.g. three months from a review of purchase invoices.	
Note. Changes in product mix over the year can also be taken into account to undermine his calculation.	
Purchase invoices	
Make sure only purchases for resale are included and check whether items such as goods for own use and ancillary items such as packaging have been excluded.	
Prices	
Where did The Taxman get his prices? In a trading account reconstruction much hinges on using the price at the time, not current prices. With the help of an actual price list can you cast doubt on the prices the Taxman has used.	
Note. You might not remember what the prices were but you can often find some supporting evidence. For example, copies of old pricing policies, price lists, analysis codes on till rolls, recommended retail prices as shown on the invoices. If you have an old price list, the Taxman will not be justified in substituting his own figures.	

The Taxman's calculations	Actioned
Is his calculation too rigid? Life is not that simple, there are many factors that can impinge on these calculations, e.g. theft and wastage to mention only two. You can expect both of these in the real world. Are the Taxman's figures the maximum achievable? Has he given credit for wastage/losses?	
Gross profit percentage Where the main activity of the business consists of the purchase and resale of goods, the Taxman will concentrate on the relationship between these two figures. The formulae most often used are: Gross profit rate (GPR) = (gross profit/sales) x 100 and mark-up rate (MUR) = (GPR/(100 − GPR)) x 100. For example, the GPR will be compared with the GPR of the same business in previous years and the GPR of similar businesses in the area.	
Other business ratios Where the business does not consist of the purchase of goods for resale, the Taxman will look for some other direct relationship between expenses and turnover to give him some indication of the reliability of the return. Examples of such ratios are fuel to takings, e.g. in the case of a taxi driver or driving instructor or food to takings, e.g. in the case of a residential home or hotel. If there is no relationship, the factors considered may include overall profitability, time spent by the proprietor and turnover expressed as an hourly/daily rate. In these circumstances put forward your own ratio that you believe best represents the business and your reasons for selecting it.	

Product mix reconstruction

In calculating adjustments required to business profits (in order to collect more tax) the Taxman uses the age-old trick of assuming that you only sell one product and at the highest price possible throughout the year. How can you prove that he is misguided?

YOU SELL MORE THAN ONE PRODUCT

One consistent way that the Taxman likes to increase the profits shown in a set of accounts is by assuming that the business only sells one product at the highest price possible. This business economics exercise is obviously flawed. As most businesses sell more than one item, the first step in challenging him on this issue is to establish the product mix for your business, i.e. the range of products sold and in what proportion. Do this for a sample period, e.g. three months, and you can generally get this information from a review of sales/purchase invoices. We've set out a **Product Mix Reconstruction** document to help you with this and to provide you with evidence to submit to the Taxman that his assumptions need upgrading.

PRODUCT MIX RECONSTRUCTION

Reconstruction

We have examined the detailed records of the business for a representative period and arrived at the following factual data about the mix of, and mark-up rates for, the products sold.

Data 1: Total purchases in the period were £78,275.

Data 2: The proportion of each product sold expressed as a percentage of total purchases (100%) is as follows:

Type of product	%
Groceries	25
Cigarettes	45
Confectionary	15
Stationery	15
Total	**100**

Data 3: The mark up on the cost of each product sold for each product type was found to be as follows:

Type of product	Mark up
Groceries	1.18
Cigarettes	1.10
Confectionary	1.25
Stationery	1.13

Our calculation of maximum achievable sales is as follows:

Product type	Purchase cost (*) £	MUR	Expected sales (**) £
Groceries	19,569	1.18	23,091
Cigarettes	35,224	1.10	38,746
Confectionary	11,741	1.25	14,676
Stationery	11,741	1.13	13,267
TOTAL	78,275		89,780

(*) Total purchases (data 1) x product mix percentage (data 2)

(**) Expected sales = purchase cost x mark-up rate (MUR) (data 3)

Conclusion

Our £89,780 is not significantly different from the total sales figure shown in the accounts (£90,000), rather than your overstated figure of £100,000 (£80,000 x 1.25).

Wastage/losses record

The Taxman typically uses a mark-up of purchases to selling price to construct an anticipated sales figure. However, this doesn't generally allow for wastage/write-offs. So what simple records could you keep about "wastage"?

WASTED STOCK

Product losses can take many forms: discounts and other price reductions made to specific groups of customers or in response to competition; special offers; annual sales and disposals for nil e.g. stock scrapped; wastage arising from spillage, breakage, processing, perishables or inexperience and pilferage by suppliers, e.g. short measures, customers or staff.

Acceptable evidence? Any diary notes kept by you during the year will assist in justifying these reductions from the maximum figures calculated by the Taxman. It can be particularly difficult to justify a figure for wastage in the absence of records. This could be established by keeping details for a sample current period using our **Wastage/Losses Record**.

WASTAGE/LOSSES RECORD

Week 1 *	Product (quantity/units lost)	Customer/member of staff	Estimated value (£)
Discounts			
Price reductions			
Special offers			
Sales			
Scrapings			
Spillage			
Breakage			
Processing			
Perishables			
Inexperience			
Pilferage/theft			
Short supplies			
Total			
Week 2 *			
Discounts			
Price reductions			
Special offers			
Sales			
Scrapings			
Spillage			
Breakage			
Processing			
Perishables			
Inexperience			
Pilferage/theft			
Short supplies			
Total			

Note

* *If there is a monthly cycle to the business then it's best to keep a record for four weeks. If it's a quarterly cycle consider keeping a record for three months.*

Reply to a business economics exercise

You might feel that the tax demand based on a business economics exercise routine is absolutely outrageous. What measured response should you give?

DON'T SAY TOO MUCH

During an enquiry into a tax return there is now a much greater willingness by the Taxman to displace the profits shown by your accounts with an estimate based on a simple business economics exercise. Using a written **Reply to a Business Economics Exercise**, try to undermine his calculations without showing your hand. Quite often what appear to be "wild" calculations are deliberate in order to get you to say too much.

REPLY TO A BUSINESS ECONOMICS EXERCISE

. . . . *(insert name)*

HMRC

. . . . *(insert address)*

. . . .

. . . .

. . . .

. . . . *(insert date)*

Dear . . . . *(insert name)*

. . . . ***(insert name and tax reference)***

I refer to your letter of . . . . . *(insert date)* received on . . . . . . *(insert date)* and note your comments.

In my/our opinion a business economics exercise cannot prove conclusively what the profits of the business were, based as it is on information supplied some years after the event. The basis of your exercise was to find an expense that had some direct relation to the income of the business. Because the scope for inaccuracies in such an exercise is so vast, I have the following reservations about your calculations not only in terms of the detailed figures used but also of the overall credibility of the ratios used.

(You then go on to attack the Taxman's calculations in detail using our checklist for attacking a business economics exercise.)

I would be grateful if you could include the amended detail in your calculations.

Yours sincerely

. . . . *(insert signature)*

Rejecting a business economics exercise

It is possible to reject a Taxman's business economics exercise approach completely, if you have reasonable grounds of course. How should you go about this?

ARE YOUR RECORDS DEFICIENT?

The Taxman's business economics exercise approach to increase taxable profits cannot be justified unless the records have been shown to be deficient in some way. He should be able to demonstrate that:

(1) There are deficiencies in the records.

(2) The results shown by the accounts are not credible.

(3) Drawings are inadequate.

The fewer of these features present, the more the Taxman's decision to base his attack on a business economics exercise should be challenged. So use our **Rejecting a Business Economics Exercise** letter if you want to negotiate this way.

REJECTING A BUSINESS ECONOMICS EXERCISE

. . . . *(insert name)*

HMRC

. . . . *(insert address)*

. . . .

. . . .

. . . .

. . . . *(insert date)*

Dear . . . . *(insert name)*

. . . . ***(insert name and tax reference)***

I/we refer to your letter of . . . . . *(insert date)*, received on . . . . . . *(insert date)* and note your comments.

My/our understanding is that a business economics exercise approach cannot be justified unless the records have been shown to be deficient in some way. You have been unable to demonstrate to my/our satisfaction that: (1) there are deficiencies in the records; (2) the results shown by the accounts are not credible; and (3) the drawings are inadequate. As these features are not present, we challenge the use of any business economics exercise in line with the decision in the Scott t/a Farthings Steak House v McDonald (HMIT (1996) SpC 381 case.

Yours sincerely

. . . . *(insert signature)*

Key events chart

If you are subject to a personal tax enquiry, deposits on your bank account statements could be taken to be a second source of income by the Taxman. However, there is an easier way of dealing with this now rather than relying on your memory, or an expensive exercise by your advisor later.

UNIDENTIFIED BANKINGS

The most common verbal explanations for unidentified bankings, or deficiencies in income when compared with personal expenditure, are: cash savings, gambling winnings, legacies, loans and gifts. The Taxman will probe any such verbal explanation. His internal manual gives guidance to inspectors on how to deal with claims relating to this type of income and advises that such claims "may sometimes be true" - which indicates the fairly sceptical approach you can expect! His line manager is also supposed to review the matter with complete objectivity and deal with each case on its merits - including how much tax they stand to collect.

Any documentary evidence you produce prior to this review has to be genuine (original documents not photocopies). Indeed, if you need to proceed to a tax tribunal, the burden of proof to substantiate such claims will rest with you, not the Taxman. If authentic detail is available, then it's not just down to hearsay.

LOG UNUSUAL INCOME

So each tax year you should review private bank statements to make sure that you have valid explanations for all credit entries. It's probably a good idea to do this anyway when preparing/signing off your personal tax return. Ideally, log unusual sources of income on a **Key Events Chart** either at the time they occur or when you are completing your annual tax return. You then have a ready explanation for the Taxman should he open an enquiry, without having to launch into a costly investigation exercise.

KEY EVENTS CHART

Date	Amount £	Business	Personal	Documentation
1983	10,000	Started	Loan from parents	Bank statement
1987	50,000	Premises acquired		Bank loan
1989	3,500		Encashed policy	Letter from insurance company
1992	25,000		Inheritance	Letter from solicitor

Private expenditure checklist

During a full enquiry by the Taxman, if your business records don't stack up, you can expect him to start asking questions about your private expenditure ("the private side"). His presumption is that any "missing" money would be reflected in a better lifestyle for you. However, you can turn this idea against him with simple summary showing how modest the "private side" is.

A FULL ENQUIRY

One of the Taxman's options is to open a full enquiry into your tax affairs, rather than just ask you about one or more aspects of a return. If matters stayed unresolved towards the end of the full enquiry, then your case would go before a tax tribunal (currently the General Commissioners). One of the things they would ask of the Taxman would be if he had taken the "private side" into account in deciding that income was missing from the business. OK, it might not come to this, but you get the picture.

So it is likely that you will need to draw up a list of private expenditure for a year (usually in the current tax year or last accounts tax year). Our **Private Expenditure Checklist** aims to cover the majority of items you should take into account.

PRIVATE EXPENDITURE CHECKLIST

Type of expenditure	£ p.w.	£ p.m.	£ p.a.	Notes
Accommodation				
Rent or mortgage				Include cost of any endowment policy
Mortgage protection				
Council tax				
Water rates and sewerage				
Gas				
Electricity				
Solid fuel				Central heating oil
Buildings insurance				
House contents insurance				
Telephone				Include private mobile phone
Repairs and redecoration				
Major alterations				Extensions/kitchens/bathrooms/ double glazing /conservatory
Household equipment and fittings				
Kitchen equipment				Cooker/fridge/freezer/ dishwasher/washing machine/ tumble dryer
Other electrical equipment				Vacuum cleaner/iron
Crockery, cutlery, glassware				
Carpets and curtains				
Bedding				
Luxury items				Sauna/solarium/billiard room
Garden				
Equipment				Tools/pots/electrical equipment
Repairs and improvements				Shed/patio/greenhouse/barbecue
Garden furniture				
Plants and seeds				Include other consumable, e.g. chemicals
Domestic and other help				
Cleaner				
Window cleaner				
Childminder				Regular babysitters
Gardener				

Type of expenditure	£ p.w.	£ p.m.	£ p.a.	Notes
Food				
Weekly expenditure				Include milk/fresh goods/freezer items
Eating out				
Take away				Include home delivery
Meals at work				
Drinking and entertaining				
Confectionery				
Clothing and personal				
Personal clothing				Work clothing
Children's clothing				School uniforms
Cosmetics, toiletries				
Hairdressing				Manicure/pedicure/massage
Transport				
Car expenses				Capital repayments/insurance/servicing/road tax/rescue services/petrol
Motor cycles				
Driving lessons				Cost of test
Home to work travel				Season tickets
Caravan				Annual charges/cleaning/capital items
Health				
Medical insurance (if paid privately)				
Eye tests and glasses				
Dental expenses				
Prescription costs				
Finance and investments				
PAYE				
Other income tax bills				
Class 2 NI				
Bank charges and interest				Credit charges/annual fees for credit cards
Life insurance				
Personal pensions				Regular premium/single premium
Regular contributions				SAYE/Tessas/ISAs
Collectibles				
Antiques				
Jewellery				

Type of expenditure	£ p.w.	£ p.m.	£ p.a.	Notes
Leisure and entertainment				
Television				Include licence
Subscription to satellite/cable				Include pay per view
DVDs/videos				Purchase and rental
Computers				Peripherals/printer/paper/internet costs
Computer software				
Games consoles				Cost of games
Music systems				
CDs tapes etc				
Books				
Newspaper and magazines				Regular subscription
Music				Instruments/lessons
Theatre/cinema				
Sport participation				Club membership/equipment/ playing fees
Sport spectating				Season tickets/periodic tickets
Hobbies				Capital and revenue costs
Education				Adult education/Open University
National Lottery				
Gambling				Horses/dogs/football pools/casino
Pets				Food/care
Holidays				
Travel costs				
Accommodation				Timeshare
Spending money				
Gifts and donations				
Presents				Special family events
Charitable giving				
Children and Grandchildren				
Schooling				Nursery/school fees/school trips
Extra curricular				Music lessons/coaching/exam fees
Pocket money				
University contributions				
Exam rewards				
Hobbies				
Weddings				
Totals				
Total private expenditure per annum	x52	x12		

Capital statement checklist

In larger investigation cases the Taxman may require a so-called "capital statement" to be prepared. What is one of these? And how can you present this to your best advantage?

WHAT IS A CAPITAL STATEMENT?

If there is difficulty in obtaining business records for earlier years, any attempt to recalculate omissions fairly precisely for individual periods will usually rely on the capital/income/expenditure reconciliation method - that is - capital statements. Any deficiencies will almost certainly be considered by the Taxman as representing diverted takings from the business. Where a surplus arises, the Taxman will regard the expenditure for that year as being too low and may have a corresponding effect on other years. (The Taxman confirms these views in his enquiry manual **EM2013** - Working an Enquiry: Reopening Earlier Years: Capital Statements.)

Every capital statement will be different but our **Capital Statement Checklist** is intended to be a guide to the types of item which must be considered.

CAPITAL STATEMENT CHECKLIST

Capital statement for . . . .*(insert name)*

Assets and liabilities as at . . . . *(insert date)*

Private income and expenditure for the period/year ended . . . . *(insert year)*

Non-business assets

Asset	Notes	Asset value (£)
Property	Private residence (watch for any changes in and ensure that expenses are picked up and any profit/loss properly dealt with)	
	Holiday home, let property, time share	
Investments		
Bank accounts	Non-business current and deposit accounts, in names of husband, wife and children	
Building society accounts - as above		
Unquoted shares		
Quoted shares		
Settlements made	(see note 4)	
Unit trust holdings		
Investment bonds		
Premium bonds		
National savings bonds and certificates		
Cash	The existence of any substantial hoards	
Loan accounts	Balances on all company loan accounts	
Loans to friends and associates		

Asset	Notes	Asset value (£)
Other assets:		
Used in the business	But not reflected on the balance sheet	
Antiques and paintings	Valuable items only	
	Normal household furnishings and antiques should be shown in expenditure in relevant year	
Cars	Vehicles held outside the business	
Boats		
Private plane		
Horses	Racing and show jumping	
Total value of non business assets		

Note 1. In all cases keep a note of the actual cost price of the asset including incidental costs of acquisition.

Note 2. Where an asset is sold during the year any profit on sale is taken to income. Any loss and incidental sale expenses are taken to expenses.

Note 3. Where unusual assets are held, make a note to pick up all running expenses and incidental income.

Note 4. Settlements should be included only where the individual retains an interest. Other settlements can be shown as expenditure in the relevant year.

Non-business liabilities

Liability	Notes	Value of liability (£)
Mortgages		
Bank loans		
Credit card balances		
Company loan accounts		
Hire purchase debts		
Loans from associates, family		
Total value of non-business liabilities		

Private income

Source of income	Notes	Amount (£)
Drawings from business		
Salary	(See note 1)	
Bonuses and commissions from employment		
Spouse's earnings		
Income from investments		
Rents received		
Interest received		
Dividends		
Proceeds from sale of assets		
Premium bond winnings		
Lottery winnings		
Cash gifts	Wherever possible large gifts should be substantiated by independent evidence	
Proceeds of life assurance policies		
Insurance recoveries		
Gambling wins		
Prize money		
Income tax repayments		
Social security benefits		
Total private income		

Note 1. If the payments are regular, under deduction of tax show the net sum received. Otherwise show the gross amount and ensure PAYE is shown as an expense (see private expenditure checklist). Watch consistency of treatment with director's loan account.

Private expenditure

Description	Notes	Amount (£)
For detail see separate checklist		
Total private expenditure		

Capital statement

	£
Balance (assets less liabilities) at start of period	
Add: Private income	
Deduct: Private expenditure	
Add net unrealised increase/decrease in market value of investments	
Balance (assets less liabilities) at end of period	

Amending a tax return

**If the Taxman considers that there's something
wrong with your tax return, but doesn't think you have been
negligent, he will normally write asking you to amend it within
30 days of his notification. If you agree with the change,
what's the most foolproof way of dealing with it?**

ALLOWED TO AMEND

At the end of an enquiry, if the Taxman finds nothing wrong with your return, he should advise you of this and write to say so in a closure notice. However, if he considers that there's something wrong with your tax return, but doesn't think you have been negligent, he will normally write asking you to make an amendment; this has to be done within 30 days of his notification. Use our **Amending a Tax Return** letter for a foolproof way to do this, which will lead to a revision of your tax liability for the year concerned, with an interest charge on any resulting underpayment or interest payable to you on any overpayment.

AMENDING A TAX RETURN

HMRC

.... *(insert your tax office)*

.... *(insert address)*

.... *(insert your name)*

.... *(insert your address)*

.... *(insert date)*

Dear Sirs

Subject: Amendment to Personal Tax Return .... *(insert tax year)*

Name: .... *(insert your name)*

UTR: *(insert the ten digit unique tax reference on the return)*

NI number: .... *(insert your NI number)*

As I filed my return on time, I am entitled to amend that return within twelve months of the filing date under s9ZA **Taxes Management Act 1970**.

This letter is to formally advise you that I have identified an entry or entries on that return that require revision. I would be grateful if you would deal with the following revision(s) as soon as possible.

Kindly change the entries on my file for:

1.................................. *(insert further information concerning an entry on your return)*.

2.................................. *(Entry "X" amended to entry "Y". Your stipulated amendment can be in the form of a narrative describing a change to contents of a particular box on that return or enclosing an amended return or an extra supplementary page or an amended supplementary page)*.

(Remember that if your change affects your tax liability you should also amend the tax due (Box 18.3) on the return.)

I would be grateful if you could acknowledge receipt of this letter and its contents.

(**Note.** If your tax liability has changed also ask the Taxman to issue a revised Tax Calculation to you.)

Yours faithfully

Request for closure letter

If you believe you've given an inspector all the information they've requested, you can ask them to close the enquiry. If they refuse, it might be because they are still on a fishing expedition or won't admit to their boss that they can't hit the targets on this case. What can you do to move things on?

ATTEMPT A NEGOTIATED SETTLEMENT

If the inspector has already dragged out the investigation, you can act, safe in the knowledge that they may be suffering internal pressure to settle one of their (by now) older cases. There is nothing to lose in attempting a negotiated settlement. Use our **Request for Closure Letter** to try and convince the Taxman to reconsider closing the enquiry. You can also threaten to have your particular case listed before a tax tribunal (currently the General Commissioners) and seek to get a closure notice imposed. Even the mention of this to the Taxman might make him reconsider his stance.

REQUEST FOR CLOSURE LETTER

HMRC

. . . .*(insert address)*

. . . .

. . . .

. . . .

. . . .*(insert date)*

Dear . . . .*(insert name)*

Request for closure of the enquiry

. . . .***(insert name and tax reference)***

Further to your last letter . . . . . . *(insert date).*

I/we now believe that I/we have provided you all the information and explanations relevant to the enquiry since it was opened on . . . . . *(insert date).*

I/we can see no further advantage for you or me/us in carrying on this enquiry and would ask you to formally close it. If you do not wish to then I/will have to consider having this matter listed before the General Commissioners and seek a Closure Notice.

I/we think it is only fair to let you know that in my/our opinion if, you do wish to keep the enquiry open this might not be seen to be reasonable or defensible should a formal complaint be made by me/ourselves.

Yours sincerely

. . . .*(insert signature)*

Official error claim

If you have made full disclosure of an aspect of your return, which the Taxman simply ignores at the time but picks up on later, whose problem is this? If it's after more than two years, then it's his problem. However, despite being fully aware of this concession, you will have to formally remind the Taxman of it in writing.

GIVEN REASONABLE DETAILS

Initially, the Taxman will look at the period covered by the return that has been the subject of the enquiry notice. In most instances there will be implications of earlier periods. The Taxman is working under the assumption that this is not the first period in which irregularities (as his manual calls them) have occurred. If he can establish the need for an adjustment for the latest period, he will have little difficulty going back to earlier periods on the basis of having made a discovery. This allows him to raise assessments for earlier income tax years or Corporation Tax accounting periods, even if he is already out of time. If you are in this situation, have a look at copies of the tax returns in question and see if you have given the relevant information on how the item was calculated. You might find that the Taxman had been given all the reasonable details he could have expected when the item first appeared but failed to check it. If you have made full disclosure of the item but the Taxman simply ignores this for more than two years, then it's his problem, not yours. He is well aware of this concession; in fact, there is a section in his manual that tells an inspector how to deal with this situation. Use our **Official Error Claim** to invoke this concession.

OFFICIAL ERROR CLAIM

HMRC

. . . . *(insert address)*

. . . .

. . . .

. . . .

. . . . *(insert date)*

Dear . . . . *(insert name)*

Arrears of tax due to official error

. . . . ***(insert name and tax reference)***

I/we refer to your letter of . . . . . *(insert date)*, received on . . . . . *(insert date)* and note your comments.

You state in your letter that it only became apparent that the *(e.g. expenses claimed were excessive)* from the . . . . . . *(specify date or tax return)* and you therefore consider this constitutes a discovery.

May I/we take issue with you on this point especially as, it is quite clear from the information disclosed within the tax returns that it drew your attention to how . . . . . . *(specify discovery item) (e.g. the expenses claimed)* were calculated/made up - [this information was given for each and every tax year in question].

Thus if you had checked my/our figures and calculations it would have appeared obvious there was an error at the time the tax returns were submitted. I/we trust you will agree that there was an error for the years in question and not fraudulent or negligent conduct on my/our part.

Just because you have now decided to look into past years' tax returns, does not mean there is a "discovery" situation.

Let me/us refer you to Arrears of tax due to official error. I/we believe the pertinent comments are:

. . . .
. . . .

"Tax will normally be given up only where the taxpayer:

a) could reasonably have believed that his tax affairs were in order and

b) was notified of the arrears more than twelve months after the end of the tax year in which the HMRC received the information indicating that more tax was due

and in exceptional circumstances

c) failed more than once to make proper use of the facts they had been given about one source of income."

I/we would therefore like this to be invoked for the tax years . . . . . *(specify years).*

Your own Enquiry Manual duly states *"if the error was obvious the information to identify it would have been made available to you".*

[I/we agree the calculations for the tax years *(specify years)* as these have been notified "in time"; two years following January 31 following the tax year.]

Please note I/we have submitted Appeal forms for the tax years . . . . . . *(specify years)* within the 30 days allowed (copies enclosed).

I/we trust we will be able to agree a basis on which to settle my appeal.

I/we await your comments.

Yours sincerely

. . . . *(insert signature)*

Enc

Obligation for past event

One tax game that's played every year-end involving getting tax relief before you've spent any money. Quite often you don't get the actual invoice in before the year-end. So instead you can include in your accounts a reasonable provision for the estimated costs of what you will eventually pay. However, what evidence would the Taxman expect to find about this?

SIGNIFICANT PROVISIONS

A reasonable provision in your accounts for the estimated costs of what you will eventually pay is an accepted accounting principle. And, as such, it is clearly recognised by the Taxman as tax deductible. However, in order to include a provision in your accounts, certain conditions need to be met under the Financial Reporting Standards. Put simply, you need a "present obligation for a past event". Use our **Obligation for Past Event** file note to fend off any challenge from the Taxman as to the legitimacy of significant provisions in your accounts.

OBLIGATION FOR PAST EVENT

File note

In our opinion the Company has a present obligation for a past event. Therefore in accordance with Financial Reporting Standard 12, we have decided to include a provision in the Company's accounts for the year/period ended . . . . . . *(insert date)*. We have examined the evidence available to us and are satisfied that this meets the conditions of FRS 12 as follows:

Condition 1. There is a current obligation as a result of a past event.

The past event was [e.g. wear and tear on the building caused by the Company's use of it] and the current obligation is [e.g. the new legislation /dilapidations clause in a lease etc.]. To be prudent we must presume that the Company will have to incur expenditure, as there is no evidence to suggest that it won't.

Condition 2. It is known that expenditure will be required to meet the obligation.

A list of things the Company has to do to meet the obligation has been prepared and costed. Part of the cost is self-evident from the fee quote prepared by the specialist consultant whom we intend to commission to prepare a detailed report.

Condition 3. A reliable estimate can be made of the expenditure.

The estimates of the costs involved have been prepared in consultation with the independent specialist consultant.

. . . . *(insert name)*

Managing/Finance Director

For and on behalf of the board of

. . . . *(insert name of company)*

. . . . *(insert date)*

Complaint letter

Ultimately, the Adjudicator's Office handles all complaints about the Taxman. However, the adjudicator will only examine a complaint if it has been through the proper levels of authority within HMRC first. It's the same letter but to different people. So what should you put in this particular piece of correspondence to the Taxman?

SET OUT YOUR GRIEVANCE

If you feel you have been unfairly treated by the Taxman, the avenues of complaint are to: **(1)** the Taxman's area director; **(2)** his regional controller; **(3)** the adjudicator; and **(4)** the Parliamentary Ombudsman. Your complaint should set out exactly what is being sought - an apology, an explanation with an assurance that it will not happen again and an itemised request for compensation. You can use our **Complaint Letter** to set out your grievance to the relevant person.

COMPLAINT LETTER

[The area director] [The regional controller]

. . . . *(insert address)*

. . . .

. . . .

. . . .

. . . . *(insert date)*

Dear . . . . *(insert name)*

Formal complaint

. . . . ***(insert name and tax reference)***

It is with regret that I/we must write to you complaining of the way in which . . . . . *(insert name of Inspector or other revenue official involved)* has acted in the handling of my/our tax affairs.

[I am/we are sure that if you were able to listen to recordings of telephone conversations between me/us and the officer concerned, including the one in which I/we allege he [swore/was intimidating/gave misleading advice/refused to take my complaint was talking at cross purposes] you would uphold my/our complaint without question. That conversation has caused me considerable worry and distress since.]

It says in [your Code of Practice . . . . . *(insert reference)*, HMRC manual . . . . *(insert reference)*, Statement of Practice . . . . . *(insert reference)*,] that you will . . . . *(insert action)*. However, in this case you have not done so.

Overall, I/we consider that my/our case has been handled very badly in correspondence. In particular it took . . . . *(insert number of weeks)* to provide me with an answer about . . . . *(insert question)*.

There were other delays in [replying to correspondence/finalising tax adjustments/ notifying me of the results of the internal technical review/replying to my request for a closure notification]. These delays added to my worry and distress over the investigation.

With this letter I am/we are seeking [an apology/an explanation/an assurance it will not happen again] and enclose an itemised request for compensation. [Included is a copy of the fee note charged to and settled by me/us from our advisor(s), reimbursement of which would be a tangible recognition (i.e. redress) for the mistakes made by yourselves].

[I have suffered direct financial loss as a result of your mistakes including £. . . . . *(insert figure)* for direct costs and £. . . . . *(insert figure)* for delayed resolution of this complaint]. [Out-of-pocket expenses were £. . . . . *(insert figure)*.]

Your Code of Practice 1 clearly states that you will pay compensation, or reimburse costs that arise as a direct result of your mistakes. You can, if you wish, make an interim payment whilst you calculate the total sum to reimburse.

Kindly acknowledge receipt of this letter and its contents as soon as possible.

Yours sincerely

. . . .*(insert signature)*

Enc

Error or mistake claim

You can amend a tax return up to the point where the Taxman's normal enquiry window is to be closed - this is some twelve months after the tax return was originally due in. However, if you've gone past that deadline, there is a special claim you can make to put things right. However, you'll need to get the wording spot on in order to avoid too much fuss from the Taxman in these circumstances.

IS YOUR CLAIM REASONABLE AND JUST?

If you need to amend a tax return out of time, make an **Error or Mistake Claim** under the **Taxes Management Act 1970**. If the Taxman agrees, he will give such relief as is "reasonable and just". However, you need to think about the following before making such a claim:

- an error or mistake claim cannot be made if the return was prepared in accordance with the practice generally prevailing at the time. It has never been the generally prevailing practice to enter a wrong figure on the return and so this rule should not block your claim

- you can't use an error or mistake claim to alter a claim for an allowance, e.g. capital allowances, taper relief etc. An entry for income or expenses is not a claim for an allowance and so this rule shouldn't block your application

- the error or mistake claim effectively gives the Taxman an opportunity to extend his enquiry period. Therefore, before submitting the claim, satisfy yourself that nothing else has been missed off the return.

ERROR OR MISTAKE CLAIM

HMRC

. . . . *(insert address)*

. . . .

. . . .

. . . .

. . . . *(insert date)*

Dear . . . . *(insert name)*

Error or mistake claim

. . . . ***(insert your name and tax reference)***

We have now had opportunity the to discuss with our . . . . *(insert e.g. new)* client . . . . *(insert client's name)* the computation supporting the . . . . . . *(insert e.g. the capital gain)* shown on their tax return for . . . . *(insert tax year)*.

We now insert an amended . . . . *(insert e.g. capital gain)* computation for . . . . *(insert tax year)* and in view of this (and of the omissions made by the previous agent) we request that you accept our amended computation. Our client wishes to formally claim error or mistake relief.

Any reduction in the . . . . . . *(insert e.g. chargeable gain)* arising from the above revision to their tax return to be governed by s.33 **Taxes Management Act 1970**. Which provides relief via repayment.

Yours sincerely

. . . . *(insert signature)*

Letter to chase a tax repayment

Most tax districts deal with taxpayers in strict alphabetical order. So if your surname begins with a "Z" you'll have quite a wait for any repayment due to you. However, our sources tell us that if you complain, you can get moved up the list. What if you want to do something other than phone the Taxman?

WRITE OR PHONE?

Telephone contact is often the quickest way to get things done, as you might get a response straight away. If you do phone, it's a good idea to make a note of the name of the person you speak to.

However, you may prefer to send a **Letter to Chase a Tax Repayment**. If you do, always show your tax office reference. Keep a copy of your letter and any other papers sent in case the original goes astray. If you write to your tax office, you might wait some weeks for a reply; the Taxman promises to reply to letters within 28 days (in normal circumstances).

LETTER TO CHASE A TAX REPAYMENT

HMRC

.... *(insert address)*

....

....

....

.... *(insert date)*

Dear .... *(insert name)*

Subject: Outstanding Tax Repayment

Name: .... *(insert your name)*

UTR: *(insert the ten digit unique tax reference on the return)*

NI number: .... *(insert your NI number)*

With reference to my self-assessment tax return for ..... *(insert e.g. 2008/9)*, submitted on ...... *(insert date)*, I am surprised that I have not yet received the tax repayment claimed.

This letter is to formally ask you to expedite matters and I should be grateful if you would issue the repayment cheque/transfer the funds to my account *[delete as necessary]* as soon as possible.

I would be grateful if you could acknowledge receipt of this letter and its contents.

Yours sincerely

.... *(insert signature)*

Notes

Notes

Notes

Notes

Notes